BEARDED DRAGONS

THE ESSENTIAL GUIDE TO OWNERSHIP & CARE FOR YOUR PET

Kate H. Pellham

© 2015

DISCLAIMER

This book is not intended as a substitute for the medical advice of veterinarian. The reader should regularly consult a veterinarian in matters relating to his/her pet's health and particularly with respect to any symptoms that may require diagnosis or medical attention.

Photos copyright respective owners, licensed through Dollar Photo Club unless otherwise noted.

Table of Contents

Chapter 1: Introduction to Bearded Dragons........9

Common Behaviors.....................................11

Bearded Dragons as Pets............................12

Live Insect Food...18

Space Concerns 18

Long-Term Commitment 19

Safety Considerations 20

Cost of Bearded Dragon Ownership...............22

Care Schedules 26

Safely Handling Your Dragon.......................29

Chapter 2: Crafting Your Terrarium 31

The Enclosure 35

Cleaning and Maintenance 39

Heat, Light, and Humidity............................40

The Photoperiod 41

The Thermal Gradient 44

UV Exposure...46

Mercury Vapor Bulbs...................................48

Incandescent Bulbs.....................................51

Natural Sunlight...52

Undertank Heaters 53

Heating Methods to Avoid 54

Substrate 54

Sand 56

Recycled paper 57

Cage liners 60

Newspaper 61

Substrates to Avoid 63

Cage Furnishings................................65

Hide Boxes 67

Basking and Climbing........................68

Collection from Nature 69

Peripheral Enclosures........................71

Chapter 3: Buying a Bearded Dragon................73

Choosing a Healthy Animal 73

Captive Bred vs. Wild Caught.............76

Gender 77

Species and Variants...........................78

Where to buy your Bearded Dragon 80

Bringing Your New Pet Home 84

Chapter 4: Food and Nutrition.......................88

How, When, and How often to Feed 98

What Should be in my Bearded Dragon's Salad?
....102

Where to get Vegetation? 105

Live Food and Protein.................................108

Other Food Options....................................118

Where to get insects 121

How, When, and How often to Feed Live Food124

Nutritional Supplements 126

Calcium Supplements.................................128

Multi-Vitamin Supplements 130

Watering Your Dragon 132

Chapter 5: Health and Breeding 134

Nail Trimming 135

Shedding...136

Brumation 137

Common Health Ailments 140

Breeding Bearded Dragons........................153

Buying a Partner 156

Introducing the Dragons...........................156

Brumation 158

Mating 159

Laying the Eggs......................................161

Incubation and Hatching...........................163

Care of the Hatchlings..............................167

Additional Resources................................170

Chapter 1: Introduction to Bearded Dragons

Bearded dragon (colloquially referred to as "beardies" by a lot of keepers) is a term used to refer to any member of the genus pogona. They're named for the "beard" of darker skin on the neck, though there are a couple species of the genus that lack this trait (known collectively as beardless bearded dragons). There are eight species of this genus, four of which are kept as pets. The most common of these species is pogona vitticeps, the inland bearded dragon. This is the species that will be familiar to you from pet stores and popular images. Inland bearded dragons grow to a length of 16-24 inches, a little over half of which is in its tail. In nature, bearded dragons can be tan or yellow in color, with darker markings of black or brown and spines on the throat and sides. In captivity, they are sometimes selectively bred for other colorations, including red, orange, and white.

Bearded dragons are native to Australia and can be found in the wild in most of the country. The inland bearded dragon lives in the deserts and scrubland of central Australia. Their natural habitat is dry, getting very hot in the daytime and relatively cool at night. Bearded dragons are cold-blooded and take heat from their environment rather than producing it internally. They gain energy by basking, usually on a rock or a tree branch, and because of this are most active during the daytime. During the cooler winter months they can be sluggish, sometimes even going into a kind of hibernation known as brumation. Because food can be scarce in their desert environment, bearded dragons have evolved to be omnivores, and in the wild will eat anything from leaves and flowers to insects, small mammals, birds, and even other lizards.

Common Behaviors

In the wild, bearded dragons are territorial and solitary animals, coming together only to mate. Dominance is based on size, with the biggest male taking the best food, territory, and females. Beardies don't vocalize and communicate with body language. The most common behavior is head bobbing. This is done by males as a display of territorial dominance; it can also be a sign of aggression, or a mating behavior, paired with foot stomping, to get the attention of a female. When threatened or angry, bearded dragons will also inflate and darken their beards to make themselves look larger as they're warding off predators. A submissive dragon will waves his front arm in a slow circle at the dominant dragon as a gesture of peace and acknowledgment of the other dragon's dominance. These same gestures are good indicators of a captive dragon's state of mind. A dragon bobbing his head or flaring his beard is telling you he doesn't want to be touched. The arm waving is less common in captivity since most dragons are kept in solitary enclosures.

Bearded Dragons as Pets

Bearded dragons have been kept in captivity since the mid-twentieth century, emerging as a popular pet in North America in the 1990s. If given proper care, bearded dragons are not prone to illness and are very receptive to human handling, making them popular among first-time lizard owners. Reptiles can make fantastic pets for the right kind of keeper, but they're not the pet for everybody. Just like with any new animal, you should do careful research into the species and realistically consider whether or not you're prepared to care for a new animal.

Even captive-bred lizards are closer to wild animals than cats or dogs—they are tame, but they are not domesticated, and understanding the difference is key to keeping a healthy, happy pet. Learn your dragon's behaviors and respect his space. In the wild, signs of injury are signs of weakness, and lizards are unlikely to show symptoms of an ailment unless it's very serious. Daily observation of the lizard's basking and feeding habits is important to catch any medical issues that do arise before they cause irreversible harm.

Bearded dragons are not a good pet for very young children. Though they're relatively low-maintenance in terms of total time investment, they do require a consistent daily schedule, and a young child is not likely to be responsible enough to tend to these needs on his own. Because they need external lighting, there's also a safety risk in letting very young kids tend to the lizard. Basking lamp fixtures can get very hot and cause serious burns. Young children should be supervised by an adult any time they're tending to or playing with the dragon. Keeping the enclosure out of reach and putting a lock on the lid are good security measures to keep everyone safe in a household with young children.

Because of their relatively recent introduction to the American pet industry, it's only within the past four or five years that correct and thorough information about proper care has become widely available, and the general public still tends to hold

14

some misconceptions about bearded dragons as pets. The most harmful of these is to think that every lizard requires the same care. Reptiles come from all areas of the world, and live in very different habitats. While all reptiles have the same basic needs—food, water, shelter, and heat—what's good for an anole is not necessarily good for a bearded dragon, and you should be wary of any advice that suggests otherwise.

Since they're closer to wild animals, some people don't think their dragons need regular veterinary care. If anything, regular vet check-ups are more important for a reptile species than they are for a mammal. As noted above, lizards are slow to show health problems, and the negative effects of poor heating, poor lighting, or poor diet are cumulative. A vet can catch issues with the lizard's care before the problems become serious. If you're not sure where to find a reptile veterinarian, you can check the online listings of the Association of Reptile and Amphibian

Veterinarians (www.arav.org). Not every vet will be a member but it's a good place to start.

Some people think of lizards as distant pets incapable of bonding with humans or showing affection. Since they're kept in terrariums and are relatively unobtrusive, some people erroneously view them more as decorations than as pets. In truth, though, a pet beardie will become a part of your family as much as your cat or dog. Dragons love to be in places where their humans are and have very distinct personalities. Though they don't require daily handling and are less prone to loneliness than pack animals, like dogs, beardies are usually quick to climb onto an offered hand or arm, and love to hang out on their human's lap or shoulder while watching TV or surfing the internet (and not just because we're warm!). Since the males especially are very territorial, it's not a stretch to say most bearded dragons are more sociable with humans than they are with their own kind. On the cuddleability spectrum, where 1 is a fish and 10 is a dog, bearded dragons are about a 6. They won't fall asleep curled up at your feet, but you'll get lots of enjoyment from taking them out to play.

Bearded dragons have a lot of advantages as pets. Since they don't produce dander, they don't trigger allergies. The dragons themselves are odor-free and noise-free. Some of the food they eat (notably crickets) can be noisy and smelly, but the live food can be kept in a garage or basement to minimize the intrusion. Bearded dragons are also relatively inexpensive in the long-term, and especially compared to other more delicate species of reptile, are incredibly low maintenance. Before rushing out and buying a bearded dragon, however, there are a few things you should consider.

Live Insect Food

Like most reptiles, bearded dragons are omnivores, and a balanced diet includes a variety of live insects. You're likely to be handling mealworms, crickets, and roaches in significant quantities. While there are some commercial bearded dragon diets available, these are not sufficient to take care of all of a dragon's nutritional needs. Don't buy a reptilian pet if you're not comfortable touching bugs.

Space Concerns

Bearded dragons are active lizards of relatively good size. Expect to buy or build an enclosure that's at least six feet square. A commercial 55-gallon glass aquarium is an acceptable size, if you're looking to get a sense of scale. You should be able to put the enclosure away from windows and doorways, avoiding drafts and direct sunlight. Keep in mind this is for one bearded dragon. Every adult dragon should be allotted six square feet of space, whether this is in separate (recommended) or shared enclosure.

Long-Term Commitment

Bearded dragons can live up to 12 years if cared for well, and have an average lifespan of 8-10 years in captivity. There's a tendency for people to buy lizards and other small animals as a kind of "consolation pet" because their current living situation doesn't allow cats or dogs. This is fine, to some extent—bearded dragons will fill your companionship needs—but make sure you'll still want to have the dragon five years down the line. Don't buy a lizard with the expectation that it'll be easier to care for than a dog or cat. The needs of a beardie are different but equally as demanding as caring for larger animals.

Safety Considerations

As mentioned above, bearded dragons require a basking lamp to thrive, and these fixtures can get very hot after being on for the 12-14 hours in a normal beardie's "day." You should be mindful of this when placing your cage. If you have other pets—especially cats—they'll likely be curious about the new creature and could burn themselves on the fixture. A wire mesh cage for your basking light (available at most reptile supply stores) will prevent burn injuries to people and pets alike.

Lizards also are known to carry certain strains of microorganisms that can be harmful to human health. The most well-known of these is salmonella, which can be carried by reptiles and causes flu-like symptoms in humans. You should always wash your hands after handling your dragon or doing any maintenance to his cage. Food and water dishes should be designated for reptile use only and not washed alongside human dishes, and the reptile's enclosure should be kept away from any food preparation areas. Some pet owners want to kiss or snuggle their animals, or share fruits and salads with them, but these practices are not recommended for reptilian pets.

Bearded dragons rarely bite. You can avoid being bitten by not handling your bearded dragon when it's making aggressive or territorial displays, like head bobbing or inflating his beard. Use caution when hand feeding, as the dragon could accidentally nip your fingers, mistaking them for food. Beardies can't cause severe injury to humans, though their bites are powerful enough to break the skin. If you do get bitten, thoroughly wash the area with warm, soapy water, apply an antibacterial ointment, and keep an eye out for infection.

Unlike other reptiles (notably snakes and arboreal lizards) bearded dragons are not accomplished escape artists and the biggest security concern with their cages is in keeping unwelcome guests out, as opposed to keeping the pet in. A covered enclosure is recommended even if you don't have any kids or other pets in the house. Dragons will eat any insect that happens to wander into its home, and these animals may be harmful to dragons, or carry parasites from being out in the wild.

Cost of Bearded Dragon Ownership

Hatchling dragons (less than six months old) tend to cost somewhere in the range of $25-$50 per individual, with breeders generally being cheaper than pet stores. Full-grown dragons tend to start at $100 for a common variety, with rarer Morphs and variants typically selling in the $100-$200 price range (more on Morphs and variants in chapter 3). Depending on what style and size of enclosure you go with, you should expect to spend in the neighborhood of $100-

$150 on the dragon's tank (including a screen lid, which you may need to buy separately). If you're building your own enclosure, this cost is significantly lower, often around $50 for materials. You'll also need specialty basking bulbs, which can be more expensive than typical light bulbs (costing around $15-$30 each, depending on the style) and a light fixture with a ceramic socket to house it (typically $25-$30). Cage furnishings (hide boxes, basking rocks, etc) are the most variable aspect of an initial enclosure set-up. Store-bought, you'll likely spend around $50 total to fully equip your dragon's cage, but many lizard keepers take items from nature for their enclosures (the steps for disinfecting a new tank furnishing are outlined in chapter 2). You should also budget for an initial veterinary appointment for your new pet. Depending on the vet and the dragon's condition, this can cost anywhere from $50-$200 or more, if the lizard has serious health issues. All told, you're looking at an initial investment of around $350-$500.

The ongoing costs of bearded dragon ownership are comparatively low. Provided you're careful when handling them, basking bulbs can last up to six months (for incandescent) or even 1-2 years (for mercury vapor) so you'll probably spend less than $50 a year on lighting. The cost of substrate (a reptile's version of bedding) varies greatly depending on what kind you use. Newspaper substrate may be free if you get lots of junk mail. Commercial recycled paper substrates are the most expensive, typically costing about $30 for the most economical, 50-liter bags, which will last you 3-4 months, depending on the size of your terrarium. Other substrate options (play sand, cage liners, etc) will cost somewhere in between the newspaper and the commercial bedding, meaning you're looking at spending, at most, $120 a year on substrate.

Food expenditures will vary depending on the age of the dragon. If you have a hatchling, he'll put away as many as 500 crickets a week. If you're buying your live food from the local pet store this could cost you upwards of $100 a week. Fortunately, you can order crickets over the internet in bulk, reducing your cost to about $20-$30 a week. As they age, bearded dragons eat more vegetables and less protein. Since their salads will largely consist of the same produce you're feeding your family, it can be hard to get an accurate estimate of weekly food costs, but to be safe expect to spend $30 per week on food, all told. These costs can also be reduced by establishing your own roach or mealworm colonies (very doable with little effort) or growing your own herbs, flowers, and greens.

Bearded dragons do best with a regular schedule of care. Before buying a bearded dragon, you should outline a schedule of care for daily, weekly, and monthly maintenance tasks.

Daily maintenance schedule

Early morning: As soon as you wake up you should turn on your dragon's heat lamp. You can buy a timer for your light fixture if you're concerned about turning his light on and off at a consistent time. Shortly after waking up you should give the dragon his daily salad, leaving it in the cage most of the day for him to pick at as he chooses.

Early evening: Remove the lizard's vegetables from the tank at least two hours before turning off his basking lamp. Bearded dragons need heat to give them energy for digestion. Food eaten too late in the day could remain in the intestines longer than it should, posing an impaction risk.

Night: Turn off the basking lamp at the end of his 12-14 hour "day." If necessary, turn on night-time heating sources.

Other daily tasks:

* Inspect the cage for waste and bits of food, spot-cleaning substrate or replacing as needed

* Wipe waste from all climbing branches and rocks

* Check temperature on both ends of the cage, making sure all light sources are in working order

* Empty, clean, and refill water bowl and return it to the cage

Weekly Maintenance Schedule

Adult bearded dragons should be given live insect food dusted with calcium powder 2-4 times per week. Keep track of when you feed insects and do it on a regular schedule.

Other weekly tasks:

* If you're using a cage liner as your substrate, you should remove and clean it weekly

* Wipe down sides of cage (inside and out) with a damp paper towel

Monthly Maintenance Schedule

Once a month, you want to do a thorough cleaning of your dragon's enclosure. This includes:

* Removing all cage furnishings to thoroughly clean and disinfect them

* Fully changing the substrate, regardless of type, and wiping down the cage bottom

* Wash and disinfect the empty enclosure

* Sweep and dust around the cage, paying special attention to power strips and outlets

Most bearded dragons enjoy being handled. When you're first getting to know your dragon, approach it slowly and gently. Don't come in from above—most of a dragon's predators in the wild come in from above, and swooping in on the dragon could cause him to panic and stress. The best way to pick up an adult bearded dragon is to slide your fingers underneath his midsection and lift up. For younger dragons, it's best to simply offer him your palm, using the other hand to herd him onto it. Once you get to know your beardie, you'll likely find he'll walk right up onto your arm when you put it in the enclosure.

Never squeeze or pinch a bearded dragon, as this could damage his lungs and internal organs. You also want to avoid picking it up by the tail. Like many lizards, bearded dragons can detach their tails when they feel threatened. While the tail will eventually grow back, it'll be discolored and stunted, and

29

breaking off the tail is painful for the dragon, leaving a wound that could get infected. You also want to avoid handling a bearded dragon for at least an hour after it's eaten. The dragon needs the heat from his basking lamp for digestion, and putting pressure on his stomach could make him throw up on you. Head bobbing and beard flaring are common "don't touch me" dragon behaviors, and you should avoid picking him up if he's making these displays.

Though they do like being handled, you shouldn't keep a bearded dragon out of his enclosure for too long. Unless your house is especially warm his core temperature will start to drop after about an hour, making him sluggish. If his skin darkens, this means he's too cold and you should return him to his home.

Chapter 2: Crafting Your Terrarium

You should set up your bearded dragon's enclosure fully before bringing the animal home. There are a few reasons for this. Primarily this is to avoid putting undue stress on your lizard. The adoption process can be stressful for any animal, not only the journey itself but also growing accustomed to its new environment and keepers. Having the terrarium ready to go means you can put your lizard into its new home as soon as possible, reducing the amount of time it's away from a basking lamp or other heat source. Prior preparation of the terrarium also allows you to test its functionality. Take a temperature reading at both the hot end and the cool end of the tank, making sure the range is suitably established and that all your equipment is functioning correctly.

Carefully consider the placement of your terrarium in your home. Glass terraria especially should be kept out of direct sunlight. Your beardie likes it hot, but the glass sides cause a greenhouse effect, increasing the enclosure's interior temperature to dangerously high levels. On the other end of the temperature spectrum, keep your dragon's cage away from drafty areas, so that it doesn't get too cold at night when his basking lamp is turned off. Light and temperature specifics are covered in more depth later in the chapter.

Bearded dragons are relatively friendly and laid-back lizards, and don't generally get stressed if housed in a room with daily foot traffic—in fact, they're highly curious animals and you may find your beardie enjoys sharing a room with his humans.

Keeping the animal in a more public area will also make sure it's getting daily attention and observation. Avoid kitchen areas—the fumes from cooking and cleaning could hurt the dragon, and from a people perspective, it's advisable to keep the lizard and all of his supplies well away from food. A family room, den, or home office would be an ideal room for your bearded dragon's cage, so long as he can still get 8-12 hours of relative darkness and quiet. If you're buying a dragon as a pet for a child, she may want to keep the lizard in her room. This is generally discouraged, unless the child is an older teen and you're sure she's responsible enough to handle the daily care. Unlike mammals, lizards can't cry for attention when they need it. If you do keep the beardie's cage in a child's bedroom, it's advisable to provide some kind of weekly schedule in check-sheet form so you know the pet is being cared for regularly and effectively.

As you're shopping for enclosures, you may be confused by all the words used to refer to them. Is an aquarium different than a terrarium? And what the heck is a vivarium? Generally speaking, these terms refer more to the purpose of the enclosure than to its construction. An aquarium is a tank or bowl built for the purpose of housing aquatic creatures, while a terrarium is meant to house terrestrial flora and fauna. Vivarium is a catch-all term for any artificial enclosure designed to simulate a natural environment. As a lizard owner, you can use any suitably-sized vivarium—whether it's marketed as an aquarium or terrarium—to house your pet. It's more the fish, amphibian, and turtle owners who have to be concerned with these distinguishing factors, as some terrariums are made with thinner glass that can't stand up to the weight of water.

The Enclosure

Bearded dragons need a good-sized enclosure to thrive. A good rule of thumb is to shop for an enclosure that's at least six square feet, with a minimum height of 15 inches. If you're shopping for pre-made glass aquaria, 55-gallon long sizes are perfect for single adult dragons. Hatchlings, of course, will have diminished space needs, and you can start them in a 10- or 20-gallon long enclosure, upgrading to a larger space when they're six months of age.

Male bearded dragons can be highly territorial. While some individuals get along with other dragons, you shouldn't count on it before you know the personality of your animal. If you're planning on keeping more than one dragon it's best to house them separately. Absolutely do not put two male bearded dragons in the same enclosure. Male dragons have been known to attack—or even kill—cage mates of both genders, so even with a breeding pair it's ideal to house them separately most of the time, bringing them together only during breeding periods or supervised play.

There are a wide range of commercial vivaria that will work wonderfully to house your bearded dragon. Glass aquaria are by far the most prevalent and have several advantages. They're durable, widely available, and easy to clean, and they come in a set range of sizes, meaning finding display shelves or replacement screen tops will be easier. Glass aquaria are relatively inexpensive and hold heat well. The downside is that glass is heavy, and a 55-gallon tank complete with lizard and furnishings can be very difficult for one person to move effectively. There are some glass terraria on the market designed specifically for use with lizards that are made from a thinner and lighter-weight material, but you should buy these with caution—the glass is thin enough that dropping the water dish on it once could shatter a side, sending you off on an emergency run to your local pet store.

Molded plastic enclosures are another popular choice for bearded dragons. These are designed as terraria and often have a sliding door on the front, rather than being open-topped enclosures, which can be a less intimidating way to approach your lizard. Though bearded dragons are not such accomplished escape artists as arboreal lizards like anoles, they may still dart out of a front-opening enclosure if you're not paying attention, meaning these cages are not recommended for households with cats or other potential predators. The main advantage of molded plastic enclosures is that they're both lightweight and durable. They're easy to clean, easy to carry, and not likely to break from standard wear and tear. The main disadvantage is that they're more expensive than standard glass aquaria, and may be harder to find at a generalized pet store—you may need to look online, at an exotic pet store, or at a reptile expo. Certain models are also poorly ventilated, especially the taller models that are designed for arboreal lizards requiring high humidity.

Wire mesh is another popular material for lizard enclosures, but isn't the best bearded dragon enclosure in most situations. Wire mesh doesn't hold heat very well, but it does provide excellent ventilation, meaning it may be a good enclosure if you live in a hot, humid area of the world. It is also the only style of cage that is compatible with providing natural sunlight to your lizard without running the risk of greenhouse heating. If you plan on giving your beardie occasional exposure to natural sunlight, you may want to keep a secondary wire mesh enclosure on hand for this purpose. Wire mesh enclosures are lighter in weight than those made of glass, but the sides of such enclosures may be harder to clean. Pre-made versions are also not widely available, though if you're handy they're relatively easy to build. The methods for doing this will vary depending on what kind of materials you're using. Step-by-step guides and designs for different styles are available online. Because they're a more specialty item, pre-made wire mesh cages tend to be the most expensive of the commercial cage options.

Cleaning and Maintenance

Your lizard's terrarium should get a thorough cleaning once a month. When you do this, remove everything you can from the cage (including your lizard) and wipe the inside down with soapy water. If you've got permanent platforms or branches installed, make sure you clean all corners, edges, and bottoms. The cage should be completely dry before you put anything back so you don't risk raising the humidity.

You can use your lizard's heat lamp to dry the cage faster. Wash all cage furnishings and food/water dishes when you do this, also allowing them to dry completely. Once everything's clean and dry you can put in fresh substrate and rebuild the tank.

Certain substrates require daily changing, and regardless of what you use, spot-maintenance should be a part of your daily routine. When you give your beardie his salad, wipe any visible waste off of branches and hide boxes and remove the soiled substrate. Keeping the enclosure clean prevents the development of bacteria or fungus that can cause potentially serious health issues.

Heat, Light, and Humidity

Being desert creatures, bearded dragons do best in an environment with high heat and low humidity. Let's talk about humidity control first, because where dragons are concerned, that's the easiest thing to address. The ambient humidity of most homes is suitable for a bearded dragon; what you're primarily concerned with is preventing humidity from building up inside the cage. Keep the water dish as small as possible and position it on the cool side of the tank, where the basking lamp won't turn the lizard's healthy drinking water into potentially harmful airborne vapor. If the dragon knocks his water over, remove any moistened substrate from the cage.

Lighting and heat can be a more complicated issue. There are three main things here you need to address: a consistent photoperiod, an effective thermal gradient, and adequate exposure to UV rays.

The Photoperiod

Photoperiod is a term referring to the amount of light a creature receives during an average 24-hour cycle. The ideal photoperiod for a bearded dragon is 12-14 hours of daylight, followed by 10-12 hours of darkness. Though the Australian outback is a temperate zone—meaning the period of sunlight is shorter in the winter than in the summer—it's not necessary to simulate this for dragons in captivity unless you plan on breeding them (there's more detailed information on breeding in chapter 5). In captivity, a photoperiod is generally created by turning the lights on in the morning and off at night. You can do this manually or buy an automatic timer for your light fixture from your local home improvement store.

Bearded dragons in the wild are accustomed to relatively cool nighttime temperatures. So long as the temperature in your house doesn't drop below 65°F, you won't need night-time heating. If your house gets cooler than that a ceramic heat emitter is the best option. They can be expensive but they're durable, lasting ten years or more. Heat emitters look like flattened opaque light bulbs, and while they'll fit a standard light socket, they generate too much heat for most fixtures to handle. For safety reasons, you should only use ceramic light sockets with heat emitters.

You'll often find bulbs in the reptile section of a pet store marked as "night bulbs." These put off a red, blue, or purplish light in addition to heat and UV radiation. These bulbs are intended for easier viewing of nocturnal pets and shouldn't be used as a night-time heating source for diurnal lizards like bearded dragons. The UV rays these bulbs put out encourage night-time basking and can throw off a dragon's metabolic rhythm.

The Thermal Gradient

Thermal gradient is a term that refers to the difference in temperature between the hot and cold end of your tank. Bearded dragons regulate their temperature externally. When they're cold, they bask in sunlight and acquire energy; when they're too hot, they retreat into the shade. As a dragon owner, you should establish a hot (basking) and a cold (shade) end within your enclosure. Put all heat sources at the same end of the cage, opposite the side where you put the water dish. Don't guess as to whether you've established a good thermal gradient—test it! The optimal basking temperature is 95-105°F, and the "cool end" should be around 80°F in the daytime. At night, both ends can safely drop to 65°F without causing harm to your lizard.

Let's take a moment to talk about thermometers. Don't bother with a thermometer that's not going to give you an accurate reading. These are at best a waste of money. This includes stick-on thermometer strips and gauge thermometers that attach to the outside of your cage. Not only can these be wildly inaccurate, but they're also not going to give you a true sense of the temperature at the basking spot—the place it's most important. Find a model with an external probe that can be exactly positioned—they're usually available at department stores, hardware stores, or electronics stores. Even better, you could get an infrared temperature gun. Not only are they highly accurate but they can take instant readings without going inside the cage. Popular among breeders, they are especially good for individuals with multiple lizard enclosures, as they allow you to temp every cage in the room without having to open a single one.

As humans, we typically talk about UV (ultraviolet) rays as a negative thing. They're the part of sunlight that contains solar radiation, and consequently the part responsible for skin cancer. Despite that dubious association, the energy provided by UV rays is responsible for formation of vitamin D within the body, a very valuable vitamin for lizards and humans alike. Vitamin D allows for proper calcium absorption, which is necessary for skeletal health. A bearded dragon that doesn't get sufficient exposure to UV rays is at a greater risk for Metabolic Bone Disease, a very painful and potentially fatal chronic condition.

Glass effectively blocks ultraviolet radiation. This means sunlight coming in through a windowpane won't contain the necessary UV rays, so even if you're using a mesh-sided enclosure, putting your dragon's cage in front of a closed window won't give him the benefits of natural sunlight (remember you should never put a glass or plastic aquarium in front of a window due to greenhouse effect—I've said it before but it bears repeating).

Some basking lamps also provide UV rays; if they don't, a separate fluorescent bulb should be installed in the cage. If you buy a commercial glass aquarium you can find fluorescent fixtures sized to fit in the fish section of your pet store (fluorescent bulbs are a common light source for fish tanks). Don't just buy any fluorescent bulb, though; not all of them produce the right kinds of UV light. Look for one with at least 5-10% UVB. If you have to install your own fluorescent fixture, make sure it's half to one-third the length of the cage. The distance of the dragon from the light is important. It's most effective when the beardie can get within one foot of the bulb, but shouldn't be close enough your dragon could touch it and burn himself. It's best to put the fluorescent bulb on the end of the tank with the basking site, since that's where your beardie will go to fill its light and heat needs. This light won't put off enough heat on its own, so it should be used in conjunction with a basking lamp or other heating option. It should be set to the same timer as your basking lamp. This style of bulb stops producing effective levels of UVB rays before it stops producing visible light, so make sure to replace your fluorescent bulb every six months, even if it still looks like it's putting out light.

Mercury Vapor Bulbs

These bulbs are very popular with lizard owners because they provide for all your lizard's heat and light needs without requiring a second fluorescent bulb. Like with the fluorescent bulbs above, look for a model that gives off 5-10% UVB. Pet stores specializing in exotic pets are the best places to find these. They'll come in a wide variety of sizes and wattages. You'll want at least a 100-watt model to get the right heat output in a 55-gallon tank, and a higher wattage for larger cages. Don't put a mercury vapor bulb in a normal light fixture. They get hotter than incandescent bulbs—especially when left on for twelve hours at a time—and they can melt the inside of a standard light fixture. Buy a heat-resistant ceramic light fixture instead. Avoid models with dimmer switches—these will also melt when a mercury vapor bulb is used in the fixture, and will ultimately malfunction.

Mercury vapor bulbs are more expensive than traditional incandescent bulbs, but they also last longer (up to two years if you don't break it) and give you the simplicity of a single light fixture. If you're using a traditional screen-topped enclosure, you can simply set the light fixture on top of the screen and position the in-cage furnishings so your dragon will always be at least 18" from the bulb. If you'd rather, most fixtures come with a clamp so you can put them on a stand and position them near the cage without touching it. This is the best option with acrylic or molded plastic cages.

A note of caution on mercury vapor bulbs: The hotter they get, the more delicate they are. When it's hot, a mercury bulb will break under the pressure of unscrewing it. Avoid handling the bulb for at least fifteen minutes after you've turned it off. This also goes for the ceramic socket it's plugged into, which is unlikely to break but is very capable of burning humans and animals alike. If you also own uncaged pets—especially cats—it's a good idea to fashion some kind of cage around the light fixture to prevent injury to curious paws and noses.

Having said that, mercury vapor bulbs are the easiest way to give your lizard all its heat and UV needs, and are what I personally use to heat beardie enclosures.

Incandescent Bulbs

Incandescent bulbs—even the ones you use in your lamps at home—can put off enough heat to give your lizard a pleasant basking temperature, though you'll need a secondary source of UV rays. The advantage of an incandescent bulb is that you can use it in a normal light fixture, and if you have a plastic cage you may find it a more convenient option. Since the fixture and the bulb won't get nearly so hot, it's a safer option for homes with small children or overly curious dogs and cats.

A note on this: Bulbs labeled as "full spectrum" are the same as regular incandescent bulbs as far as your lizard is concerned. The spectrum they're referring to is the visual spectrum and does not include ultraviolet wavelengths. If you use a full spectrum bulb for heat, you'll need another source of UV.

Natural Sunlight

If you live in an area of the world that makes it possible, taking your dragon outside for some natural sunlight can be a fine supplemental source of heat and UV rays. A glass or plastic enclosure should not be used for this purpose because of the greenhouse effect mentioned above. Even if you're using a wire mesh enclosure, you may find it easier to build a smaller cage for your back patio (or wherever you'll be taking your beardie for fresh air) than to move your full cage in and out. Unless you live in a true desert you shouldn't count on natural sunlight as your main source of heat and light, instead taking your dragon out only for brief, supervised excursions.

Undertank Heaters

Undertank heaters are a functional but sub-optimal way of providing heat in an adult bearded dragon's enclosure. They can be positioned on one side of the tank to create a suitable thermal gradient, though you have to be very careful with where you put them. Dragons that get too close to the heater can easily burn themselves, and you have to be especially cautious if you're using substrates like sand and recycled paper that encourage a beardie's natural burrowing behaviors. Undertank heaters can be useful is as an alternative night-time heating source that's less costly than a ceramic heat emitter.

Don't use heat rocks (also called hot rocks or sizzle stones) for bearded dragons. Sometimes found in the pet store's reptile section, hot rocks consist of a heating coil surrounding by resin meant to look like a stone. The problem with these devices is that they don't resonate heat well, meaning your dragon will only be at its ideal temperature if it's standing directly on top of the rock. Thin spots can also develop in the resin over time, resulting in exposed heating coils that could cause serious burns. Heating tape is also not recommended for bearded dragons because it has a tendency to spread heat unevenly and can be difficult to regulate.

Substrate

The substrate in a lizard's cage is different than the bedding you'd give to a rodent. The main purpose of substrate isn't to provide nesting material but to give your lizard some purchase as he's walking around his cage. The claws and pads of a lizard's feet don't do well on smooth surfaces. A bearded dragon raised walking on a glass aquarium bottom will develop an unnatural gait that may affect its ability to catch prey. Substrate also absorbs your lizard's waste and catches any spilled food or water, making it easier to keep the cage clean.

The main concern with the substrate, from a health perspective, is to avoid causing impaction. Gut impaction is caused by foreign material getting lodged in a lizard's stomach and can be a serious ailment, sometimes requiring surgery. Because of the risk of impaction, some substrates normally recommended for lizards are unsuitable for bearded dragon enclosures, including gravel and crushed walnut shells, as well as any kind of soil, bark, or mulch. In fact, most of the commercial substrates—even those designed for reptiles—aren't suitable for bearded dragons, and some of the best options don't come from a pet store.

Sand

Play sand (like you would put in a child's sandbox) is one of the best substrate options available. This is different than the bagged sand substrates in the reptile section; those sands are calcium-based and could clump in a beardie's stomach, making them an impaction risk. Play sand, though, is made of fine enough particles to pass safely through a lizard's stomach if eaten. It also is the most natural-looking substrate if you're trying to simulate your beardie's natural desert environment. It holds heat well, and allows lizards to burrow. The main disadvantage of sand is that it's heavy, especially in the quantities needed for an adult's enclosure, and it can make your terrarium difficult to move.

If you're using sand, cover the bottom of the enclosure to a depth of about three inches. Play sand substrates can be spot-cleaned. Remove areas containing lizard waste or spilled food and water on a daily basis and you should only have to swap out the entire substrate monthly. Undertank heaters shouldn't be used with sand substrates. The heat they produce doesn't penetrate the sand well, and to achieve the right heat levels you'd have to crank it up so much the beardie could burn himself when he burrows.

Recycled paper

More often found in the small animal section of the pet store, recycled paper bedding can make a great substrate for lizards, as well. Depending on the brand, it can look like paper tufts or shredded paper, and the color options range from dingy gray to off-white to paper-towel brown—not the most aesthetically pleasing choice, but it's highly absorbent, odor-free, and allows dragons to burrow. Avoid the compressed pellet form of this bedding as it could be an impaction risk. The main advantage of recycled paper over sand is that it's lighter, making your cage easier to move.

As with sand, you should fill the bottom of the tank to a depth of three inches and avoid using undertank heaters. It can also be spot-cleaned and should be fully replaced once a month. Recycled paper is a less suitable substrate for hatchlings—it's so absorbent it poses a dehydration risk. It's also compostable, and flushable in small quantities.

Commercial recycled paper substrates can be expensive, but you can also make your own out of old sheets of paper. You can use junk mail for this if you sort out glossy pages, the sticky parts of envelopes, and any non-paper (plastic windows, staples, etc). Tear the paper sheets in half and soak in a large container of lukewarm water. Move them around with your hands, tearing into smaller and smaller chunks, until the soaking water is too grey to see your hands. At this point, drain the paper, then return it to container and re-fill with water. Do this four or five times, then put the paper in a colander and rinse it until clear water runs out when you squeeze it. Form the pulp into baseball-sized blobs, break them up into scraps, and allow them to dry. This process can be time-consuming in the quantities you'll need but it's an eco-friendly and cost-effective alternative, and could be a fun project to do with young children to make them feel like they're part of the lizard's care.

Cage liners

Commercial cage liners are reusable mats that you can find in the reptile section of the pet store. They're cut to fit the standard terrarium sizes so if you're using a store-bought enclosure you can probably find one that's the exact dimensions you need. The advantage of a cage liner is that it's lightweight and simple, with no mess from filling the cage. It also should fit flush with the edges of your terrarium, leaving no place for crickets to slip underneath and hide. They come in a variety of colors and styles, making them more aesthetically pleasing than newspaper or recycled paper. The disadvantage is that they don't allow your lizard to burrow.

Cage liners can't be spot-cleaned, though they are machine washable. Keep a couple cage liners on hand so that you can put a fresh one in as soon as you remove the soiled one to clean it. Unfortunately, you'll have to take out the entire liner every time you clean the cage, which—depending on the complexity of your cage furnishings—may be a hassle. Since they can't be spot-cleaned, cage liners should be changed weekly, at the least, and more often if your lizard is especially messy. Wash dirty liners in hot water to kill all bacteria unless the manufacturer's label specifies otherwise. Cage liners are a good substrate option for hatchlings.

Newspaper

A popular and inexpensive choice, newspaper is the preferred substrate of most breeders because of its simplicity and wide availability. It has similar aesthetic drawbacks to recycled paper and is less absorbent than the three options above. Keep an especially close eye on crickets fed to your beardie when you're using newspaper as a substrate—they like to hide under the edges and can come out later and attack your lizard. Beardies can't burrow in newspaper, but they may pull it up and slip underneath, so it's a good idea to put it down in a few layers.

Newspaper can be spot-cleaned to a point by tearing out strips and patches, but you'll probably still find yourself replacing the entire substrate several times a week. Glossy papers aren't as absorbent and shouldn't be used as substrate. There's no evidence that the ink in newspapers is harmful to animals; if you're concerned, you can buy rolls of fresh newsprint from most arts and crafts stores. Plain brown paper towels or butcher paper can also be used in the same way. Like cage liners, newspaper is an excellent substrate for hatchling dragons.

A lot of coffee shops provide newspapers for their customers in the morning and then throw them away the next day. See if the baristas at your local café would be willing to save you some old papers if you need extra for your dragon's cage. You can pick them up with your morning coffee.

Substrates to Avoid

It was mentioned above, but it bears repeating: Don't use any wood, mulch, or soil-based substrates with your bearded dragon. Aside from the impaction risk, the oils in wood tend to irritate bearded dragon skin. Anything containing cedar is especially bad. The same compounds in cedar that make it a natural insecticide and give it that good smell are very toxic to lizards, causing skin lesions and respiratory issues that mimic other common lizard ailments and often go undiagnosed until it's too late.

Avoid any substrate that's pellet-shaped, or comprised of particles larger than sand. Your dragon is almost guaranteed to consume small amounts of its substrate at feeding time, and you should avoid anything that may cause impaction. Alfalfa pellets are especially bad. They're an ideal breeding ground for fungus and bacteria, and beardies not only eat them accidentally—they tend to love the taste.

Finally, if you're using any kind of a single-sheet cage liner, make sure it's a flat, unbroken surface with no stray loops or fraying edges. Don't use traditional carpeting; the small threads can catch a beardie's toes, causing injury. The same goes with artificial turf, which should also be avoided.

Bearded dragons are curious lizards, and they do a lot of their exploring with their mouths. Keep this in mind when you're selecting cage furnishings. Whatever it is that you put in your beardie's cage, assume he's going to try to eat it, and when he can't, he's going to climb on it.

Wood can be a great furnishing material as long as you're careful about what kind of wood you use. Cedar is toxic to lizards, as I said above, and it's generally a good idea to avoid all conifers, including pine, juniper, hemlock, and yew, as these contain similar compounds that may cause skin and respiratory issues. Approved woods for bearded dragon enclosures include oak, dogwood, aspen, and maple. Flowering and fruit trees can be good materials, as well. Double check with the experts at your local exotic pet store (or those on online forums) before putting other wood species in the cage.

Stone and clay are also safe, durable materials for cage furnishings. They hold heat well and make great basking spots. Walking over stone also helps a dragon to keep his claws filed down to a safe length. Make sure to file down any sharp edges and avoid rocks that flake or crumble, as the small fragments could be an impaction hazard. If you use porous rocks, like sandstone, keep them away from the water dish. They absorb water readily and could be a source of extra humidity. Plastic, plexiglass, and acrylic can also be fine cage furnishing materials, as long as they're non-toxic and hard enough your dragon can't take a bite of them. If you notice nibble marks in the plastic, remove the item and replace it with something hardier.

A lot of people want to put plants (either live or artificial) in their terraria, but this is not recommended with bearded dragon enclosures. The substrates that are best for bearded dragons won't grow live vegetation, and since the lizard loves climbing, potted plants are likely to topple. Also remember that what's décor to you is dinner to your dragon and isn't likely to last long. Live plants also produce moisture, which can raise the humidity level inside the enclosure to unhealthy levels. Fake plants may work, but avoid anything that has cloth or silk leaves and remove the plant immediately if you notice nibble marks.

Hide Boxes

Even highly social lizards like bearded dragons want to get out of the spotlight once in a while. Hide boxes provide your lizard with a cool, dark place to escape to when he's had enough heat. You should have at least two places to hide in the enclosure, one on the basking end and one on the cool end. An effective hide box is large enough your lizard can turn around inside of it. The opening should allow the dragon to enter and exit easily without letting in excess light. Cork bark is a popular material for hiding spaces, and you can find a lot of attractive stone designs at pet stores.

Basking and Climbing

Bearded dragons are natural climbers and a few well-placed angled branches or stone piles will make your pet very happy. At the very least, you'll need one under the heat lamp to serve as a basking spot. Stone works great for this because it will absorb the heat from the lamp and diffuse it slowly into the evening, but if you use a branch (instead or in addition) make sure it's not up so high that the dragon can come into contact with any lights or fixtures. Basking branches should be a bit bigger in diameter than the width of your dragon.

If you're using sand or recycled paper substrate, make sure to put all cage furnishings on the bottom of the enclosure, under the substrate, so the dragon can't burrow beneath and make them topple. If you're stacking stones, you should seal them together so they don't fall over. You can use aquarium sealant for this, provided the stones are clean and dry. You can also use aquarium sealant to attach larger branches to the sides of the tank.

Collection from Nature

If you see a stone or branch on the ground that would be perfect for your beardie, there's no reason you can't bring it home to him, provided you take a few simple safety precautions. With branches, always make sure you identify the type of wood and double check that it's not toxic. Also remove any crumbling bark, pointy branches, or thorns. With stones, check to make sure there are no crumbling edges. Bring the item home and wash it with soap, using a toothbrush to get into all the nooks and crannies.

Anything that comes in from the outside has to be disinfected to remove any parasites and micro-organisms calling it home. You can do this with heat or bleach. To disinfect with heat, pre-heat your oven to 250°F and wrap the cleaned and dried item in aluminum foil. Bake it for 30-60 minutes. Let stones sit for a while before unwrapping the foil—rock retains heat well and could burn you even after the foil seems to have cooled. To disinfect with bleach, immerse the item completely in a 10% bleach solution for fifteen minutes, then remove, rinse with cold water, and allow to dry. Repeat the rinsing and drying process until you can no longer smell any bleach on the item.

Aside from your beardie's main tank, you may find it helpful to have a smaller secondary enclosure on hand. This mini-cage can be a place to put your beardie while you're cleaning his tank and can also be useful in transporting your dragon to and from the vet. If you plan on breeding your dragon, this secondary enclosure can also serve as an incubation space for eggs and, later, a home for some of the hatchlings.

Bearded dragons are omnivores and should be fed live insects as a part of their diet. That means you also have to set up a place for this live food to live. Different insect species require different

71

environments; you can find more detail on insect

homes later in the book. Depending on where your

dragon's cage lives, you may want to keep the food in

a separate room. Crickets, especially, can be

obnoxious when housed in a living space, and your

guests might not be too keen on watching roaches

squirm in a cage while they watch TV.

Chapter 3: Buying a Bearded Dragon

You've evaluated your living space and lifestyle and decided a bearded dragon is the pet for you. The terrarium's set up, the heat lamp is on, and all you need to do now is find your perfect pet. So which one is right for you?

Choosing a Healthy Animal

Your primary concern when shopping for any pet should be selecting an animal that's healthy and well-nourished. Before you buy a dragon you want to pick it up and inspect it. The dragon's skin should be sleek and taut. Baggy skin and wrinkles are often signs of malnutrition and dehydration. The lizard should also be moving easily within its cage, and not dragging any hindlimbs, as this is a sign of Metabolic Bone Disease. Check the skin for any unusual swellings or discolorations, and make sure there's no discharge coming from the eyes or nostrils. The dragon should be curious and responsive when it's taken out of its enclosure, not skittish or aggressive. If it's nipping at your fingers, this could be a sign it's not getting enough food, or that it hasn't been handled enough to be acclimated to people—both things that could lead to difficulties down the line. Also look at the enclosure the dragon's being kept in. If it's dirty and overcrowded, that's a likely sign that this dragon hasn't been receiving the best care and may develop health issues.

Lizards are very good at hiding what ails them. If a bearded dragon is acting sluggish or showing other signs of an illness this means it's advanced too far for the dragon to hide it, and it may be serious. Remember the business aspect of the pet trade before giving in to the temptation to rescue a sick dragon. Buying this lizard means giving the store owners your business, which will only encourage them to continue mistreating animals. It's better to give your patronage to a reputable store or dealer that cares well for its animals. If you feel you could care for a sick lizard and want to rescue an ailing beardie, check for reptile rescue organizations in your area. Adopting from them saves a lizard life without giving money to bad businesses.

It used to be that the majority of reptiles kept as pets were captured in the wild and then sold to distributors. While this is still the case for some species, beardies are popular pets, bred in significant numbers around the world. In fact, unless you live in Australia, you shouldn't be able to find any wild caught bearded dragons for sale. Australia's strict animal export laws have forbidden the sale of wild caught dragons for the pet trade since the 1960s, and any dragon obtained through legal channels will be captive bred—which is good news, because captive-bred animals make better pets. Since they're around both people and other lizards from the time they're born, they tend to be less territorial and more sociable than wild lizards. Captive-bred animals are also healthier, since wild caught lizards are almost guaranteed to have some kind of internal parasite.

Gender

Both male and female dragons make great pets. Males do tend to be more territorial and may be more aggressive. Females are more docile but are prone to more health issues. Egg binding is a serious concern for a female bearded dragon, and since female dragons may still produce eggs even with no males in the area, you can't be guaranteed to avoid it just because you don't plan on breeding her.

It can be difficult to tell the difference between male and female hatchlings; distinct differences don't start developing until they're at least three months old. Once they're adults, male dragons are noticeably larger and have a more pronounced beard. If you can't tell for certain or don't have another dragon for comparison, you can find out for sure by checking the base of the tail. Hold your dragon gently against a flat surface and lift the tail up slowly until it's almost at a 90° angle to the body. Look at the base of the tail. If there's a triangular bump, the lizard's female. If there're two oval shapes with a dip between them, it's a male.

Species and Variants

There are four species in the genus *pogona* that are kept as pets. The inland bearded dragon (*pogona vitticeps*) is the most common. If you see a pet in a store just marked "bearded dragon" with no qualifiers, it's more than likely an inland. These are the best dragons to keep for first-time lizard owners and the ones vets will be most familiar with.

The eastern bearded dragon (*pogona barbata*) is similar in appearance to the inland, though it's a bit larger and tends darker in coloration. Since they hail from the coasts of Australia, eastern bearded dragons are better adapted to a cool or moist environment and may be a better choice if you live in an especially humid region. The other species of *pogona* you can find as pets are beardless bearded dragons (*p. minor* and *p. brevis*). Both are smaller than inland bearded dragons but require the same basic habitat and nutrition.

In the bearded dragon community, individuals bred to emphasize a specific physical trait are known as Morphs. Dragons can be selectively bred for size, or to have smoother skin, smaller side spikes, or no spikes at all. The flashiest and most popular Morphs are alterations of the dragon's color. Hypomelanistic (or "Hypo") Morphs are significantly lighter in color, while Leucistic Morphs produce no pigment at all and are a stunning shade of pure white. Red, yellow, and orange Morphs are also popular. These specially-bred dragons tend to cost a bit more (in the neighborhood of $100-$200 dollars, depending on the Morph, compared to the $30-$100 range of a standard inland bearded dragon) and are rarely available at pet stores, requiring a trip to a breeder or reptile expo.

Where to buy your Bearded Dragon

Pet stores

Pet stores are the most convenient place for most people to buy bearded dragons. Most shops sell dragons that are 2-4 months old, potentially too young to correctly identify the gender, though some stores might have adult dragons as well. Buying from a pet shop is generally a little pricier than buying directly from a breeder, and the staff of multi-species pet shops rarely can be trusted for their reptile knowledge. They're unlikely to know anything about the dragon's origins or upbringing. Depending on where the pet store gets its reptile supply, it may be limited in the winter and early spring, when shipping of live reptiles can be costly and potentially harmful to the animals. As mentioned above, make sure that you're allowed to personally inspect the individual dragon you're buying, and check for overcrowding in the cage, which is common in large pet stores that don't specialize in reptiles.

Breeders

You can find directories online of bearded dragon breeders in your area. It's getting more and more common to find breeders listing their dragons on the internet and offering to sell and ship them to you overnight. Even if pictures are provided, you should not go this route unless you know the breeder. Most breeders who ship animals will only guarantee that the lizard will arrive alive, and you won't get a chance to really inspect your animal until he's already in your home. Breeders will be generally more knowledgeable about bearded dragon care than pet store staff, and will probably also be able to point you in the direction of a good reptile veterinarian, or give you detailed pointers about your dragon's care. They may also have certain Morphs, or at the least a wider range of individuals available.

Herp shows or herp expos

If you live close to a major metropolitan area, chances are you can find a herp expo happening nearby in the coming months. These gatherings are trade fairs for breeders and lovers of reptiles and amphibians and are a great place to find pets, live food, and reptile supplies. Since there will be multiple breeders in attendance, herp expos give you the best chance of finding specific Morphs or non-traditional bearded dragon species. These events tend to get pretty busy, so a breeder at the expo may not have as much time to answer your questions as if you visit her shop, but if you know what you're looking for this can be a great place to get it.

Reptile rescue organizations

As the number of people keeping dragons as pets has increased, so, too—unfortunately—has the number of dragons abandoned by their owners who need loving homes. You can find listings of such rescue organizations on the internet, and will be generally more likely to find such places in or around major metropolitan areas. Animals that you adopt may have been poorly treated in the past, either through ignorance or neglect, and this can make them more challenging as pets than dragons bought from a breeder. They may have chronic health or behavioral issues that never entirely go away. On the other hand, they may adapt quickly to your care and come to be perfect pets who are with you for a long time. If you're an experienced reptile owner and want to help a lizard in need, reptile rescue organizations can be a great way to do this.

Bringing Your New Pet Home

The pet store or breeder will probably give you the lizard in a hinged container or cloth bag, and you should leave him in this container until you get home. Darkness is calming for a lizard, and that's important during the stressful moving process. Bring a large cooler with you. The inside of your car is one of the worst environments for a lizard, too hot in summer and too cold in winter, and the cooler will help insulate him from this environment. Place the entire container inside with padding around it to keep it from shifting (being careful not to cover the container's air holes). A large cardboard box will do if you don't have a cooler, lined with towels or a blanket for insulation if it's a cold day.

You don't want to make any other stops between buying your bearded dragon and going home, and you certainly don't want to leave the lizard alone in the car for any length of time. On cold days, have the car warmed up before bringing the lizard out to minimize the shock of the cold air. If it's summer, make sure the cooler with your dragon inside is not in direct sunlight.

Once you get home, you want to settle your beardie into its cage. You should open the container and herd the dragon into the cage, rather than lifting him out. The containers the dragons are sold in are relatively small and he may feel cornered and nip at you, especially after his stressful moving day. If you have to pick him up, move slowly and be gentle. Once he's in the cage, don't bother your dragon for the first day or so except to feed him, giving him time to settle into his new home.

It's always a good idea to take a new pet to the vet. This is especially true with lizards because of their propensity to suffer in silence. You can ask the vet any questions you still have about the dragon's care and make sure you're on the right track. Taking your lizard in for an early check-up also lets you get to know the closest reptile vet, so if something does go wrong down the line you're not scrambling trying to find someone who can see him.

Finally, if you have other pets—especially other pet lizards—you don't want to let them interact with your new beardie for the first couple of weeks he's in the house, and preferably not until after his vet appointment. Even captive bred animals can be carrying parasites or other ailments that could spread to the healthy animals in your house. Always wash your hands carefully before tending to your other pets

if you've been touching your new bearded dragon.

Chapter 4: Food and Nutrition

Bearded dragons are omnivores, meaning they need both vegetables and meat (typically insects) to ensure their good health and longevity. Dragons in the wild have a diverse diet, being hunters more of opportunity than of taste. In addition to the worms, insects, spiders, and vegetation you'd expect them to eat, wild dragons will eat small rodents, other lizards, snakes, and scorpions. Variety is key to a dragon's diet. For this reason, canned "complete diets," even those advertised to use with bearded dragons, should not be relied upon for long-term exclusive use. They won't harm the dragon, and may be a good thing to keep on hand for the days you don't have time to mix a salad (or to ease the life of a pet-sitter while you're on vacation) but they won't provide for the dragon's long-term nutritional needs.

A dragon in the wild will have a diet consisting of more proteins, with as little as 20% of his calories coming from vegetable matter. Keep in mind, however, that what's good for a wild animal is not necessarily the best for a pet. Captive dragons are generally less active than their scrubland counterparts and don't need to stockpile energy supplies inside their body for periods of drought or famine. They also don't need to worry about evading predators, and are far less likely to be injured and need extra protein to recuperate. The exact ratio of vegetables to protein that's best for a given beardie in captivity depends on the age, gender, and health of the individual lizard. Most adult bearded dragons will do best with a diet that's about 50-75% vegetables. Hatchlings and juveniles should receive a higher protein allowance, with up to three-quarters of their diet consisting of insects.

Most bearded dragons are not picky eaters and will eat whatever they're offered, up to and including any plants in their terrarium (whether or not they're real). Rescued beardies are the notable exception to this—if they were reared and kept exclusively on insects, they might have difficulty identifying plant matter as food. Wiggling a few leafy greens in front of the beardie at feeding time to simulate an insect motion will likely get him to bite. Alternatively, mix mealworms or roaches in with his dish of greens to entice him to eat them. Flowers, fruits, and other good-tasting treats can also help teach a rescued dragon to eat his vegetables.

A responsible pet parent never lets her dragon make its own nutritional decisions. Just like with a child, a beardie may pick out the pieces of his salad he finds most appetizing and leave the rest. If you notice this happening, cut up the salad into smaller pieces and mix it together well so the beardie can't pick and choose. The negative effects of poor nutrition are cumulative and can cause long-term health problems, the effects of which are often not apparent until irreparable harm has been done.

Obesity is a major concern in adult bearded dragons, and just like in humans, an obese dragon can develop serious health problems if left untreated. In the wild, a bearded dragon can never be sure where his next meal will come from, and is adapted for "feast or famine" conditions. They have a large stomach capacity and store fat efficiently, traits that are necessary for survival but can become a problem for the pet dragon. Don't give a beardie free access to food and expect him to self-regulate his intake. Instinct means he will keep eating, storing fat for future periods of scarcity that won't be coming. Limit foods with a high sugar and fat content—like fruit or pinkie mice—to occasional treats for an adult (they can be given more often to hatchlings, who use the extra calories to build their rapidly-growing bodies). Gravid females should also be given extra food while carrying eggs and for the week or so after laying.

Calcium is important for a bearded dragon. Dragons deficient in calcium are prone to develop Metabolic Bone Disorder (MBD) which causes the limbs and jaw to warp and can affect a dragon's gait and ability to eat. Calcium supplements are the easiest way to make sure your dragon is getting as much as it needs. Look for a supplement with a calcium to phosphorus ratio of at least 2:1, as phosphorus can inhibit calcium absorption. With the right foods and supplements in the correct balance, bearded dragons thrive in captivity—so let's take a more in-depth look at just what those right foods are.

Vegetables, fruits, and other plants

Unless you live in Australia, you will probably not be offering your beardie the exact same kind of vegetation it would eat in the wild—and that's okay! The vegetables, fruits, and flowers you can find in your supermarket and garden are equally as capable of providing your beardie with the right nutritional balance. A fairly comprehensive chart of what's okay and what's not, vegetation-wise, is included at the end of this section. You may want to photocopy this and bring it with you on grocery trips.

First, let's talk about what not to feed him. Some common human foods are very bad for beardies. Avocado is highly toxic to most lizards, and can cause cardiac failure and death. Rhubarb damages a lizard's kidneys by causing calcium oxalate crystals to form, even. Members of the onion and garlic family cause digestive issues that lead to serious illness. Wild mushrooms may contain fatal liver-damaging toxins, and even those safe for humans to eat could damage a beardie's smaller body. Non-fatal mushrooms are still high in phosphorus, making them poor dragon food, and it's best to skip the fungus entirely. Some garden flowers have a known toxicity; they're listed in detail in the food chart. Finally, avoid all canned vegetables, as they're high in sodium and other preservatives that may be harmful in the long term. If possible, it's best to avoid frozen fruits and vegetables as well. The blanching process that happens before commercial freezing destroys some of the food's vitamin B1 (thiamin), a lack of which can cause muscle tremors, a condition known as hypothiaminosis.

Aside from those foods that will directly harm your dragon, there are some that should be used carefully or sparingly. If you're feeding him apples, be sure you remove the seeds, which contain trace amounts of cyanide—not enough to harm a human, but enough to be bad for smaller critters. It's generally best to avoid plants from the genus *brassica*. Foods of this genus contain high levels of goitrogens, which inhibit iodine intake and can cause thyroid problems. Notable exceptions to this rule include collard and mustard greens, which are nutritionally dense and comparatively low in goitrogens, making them great dragon chow. You also want to limit your use of foods high in oxalic acids, as these can prevent your bearded dragon from absorbing the calcium he eats. This includes beets, parsley, and spinach. Avoid foods high in phosphorus (like corn and potatoes) for the same reason. Lettuces and cucumbers have a high water content and a low nutritional density, so while they don't contain any harmful compounds, they shouldn't make up the bulk of a dragon's diet.

Fruits can be tricky to feed to a bearded dragon. They can provide the dragon with vitamins and minerals it has a hard time getting otherwise, but their high sugar content makes them an obesity risk if given too often. Fruits with a lot of acid can upset a dragon's digestive system. Use caution with tomatoes, feeding him only small pieces until you're sure how his stomach will react. Just like with vegetables, limit the consumption of fruits high in oxalic acid (grapes and pears) or phosphorus (bananas). Berries are some of the best fruits to feed beardies because they're high in fiber and vitamin C. Cranberries are especially great due to their excellent calcium to phosphorus ratio. Remember to always remove any pits or seeds the fruit has, as these are both a choking and an impaction hazard.

So what can a bearded dragon eat? The best options are leafy greens, and these should comprise the bulk of your beardie's vegetative diet. Choose varieties that are high in calcium and low in phosphorus, like endive and collard greens. Most people don't think of herbs as leafy greens because they're used more as seasoning in human cooking, but to a lizard they're simply leaves of plants, and herbs like basil, cilantro, and mint are both delicious and beneficial. Winter squashes are an excellent source of B vitamins and also have lots of potassium, fiber, and iron. If you're looking to more closely replicate the scrublands diet of a bearded dragon, cactus pads are an excellent choice. Also called nopales, cactus pads are the leaves of the prickly pear and are common in Mexican cuisine. If they're not available at your usual supermarket, check out any Hispanic grocery stores in the area. The fruit of this plant—the prickly pear, or cactus fruit—may also be available, and is also great to feed your dragon.

There are some plants a human wouldn't consider edible which suit a bearded dragon's tastes and diet. Among them are some we tend to think of as weeds. Dandelions and clover are high in nutrients but low in oxalates, and beardies can eat both the roots and the flowers. Hibiscus and nasturtium are also fairly nutritionally dense. Flowers, like fruits, should be given to dragons as treats, and not make up too much of a dragon's diet.

How, When, and How often to Feed

When preparing the salad for your beardie, aim to include 2-3 types of greens and 2-3 types of other vegetation, with as much variety as possible. For adults, only include fruit and flowers once or twice a week; for hatchlings, you can include them as often as three or four times. Grate any harder foods, like squashes and carrots. Cut other foods into bite-sized chunks. Remember, we're talking your dragon's bite, not yours! Smaller is always better. Be careful to remove any spines, pits, seeds, or other hard protrusions as these could be impaction risks if consumed.

Hatchlings under six months old should be provided with a constant supply of leafy greens. Make sure the food is served in a container shallow enough for the little beardie to get in and out. You can find a variety of shallow bowls at your local pet store, or use a small plate or the saucer from a potted plant. Leafy greens can also be hung from cage furnishings to simulate real branches in the wild. The food supply should be replenished as needed until the end of the "day" when you turn the heat lamps off, at which point any of the day's food that remains should be removed and thrown away.

Juveniles and adults should be given one serving of vegetables per day, consisting primarily of leafy greens. Designate one dish for the bearded dragon and do not use it for people food to avoid cross-contamination. You can give your dragon his salad in the morning when you turn on the basking lamp. He'll wake up, get some energy, and dig into his breakfast about half an hour later. Remove the food about two hours before you turn off the basking lamp for the day so your beardie has enough time to digest whatever he's eaten.

A lot of dragon owners want to hand-feed their pets, especially when giving them treats. This is perfectly fine to do with adult dragons, just make sure to keep your fingers out of his way—he might think they're food, and dragon bites can hurt. If you do get bitten, calmly return your dragon to his enclosure to finish his meal and wash the wound thoroughly before applying disinfectant.

What Should be in my Bearded Dragon's Salad?

Bad (toxic or unsuitable)	Okay (feed sparingly)	Great (everyday options)
Fruits	Fruits	Fruits
Grapefruit	Apples (remove seeds)	Cranberries
Lemons	Bananas	Blackberries
Limes	Cactus fruit (prickly pear)	Blueberries
Oranges	Figs	Strawberries
Flowers and herbs	Grapes	
Bluebonnets	Kiwi	
Boxwood	Melons	
Chives	Papaya	Flowers and herbs
Chrysanthemum	Peaches/Nectarines	Basil
Crocus	Pears	Cilantro
Hyacinth	Starfruit	Clover
	Tomatoes	

(terrestrial)

Hydrangea

Ivy

Lilies

Mistletoe

Morning glory

Poinsettia

Rhododendro

n

Vegetables

Avocado

Garlic

Mushrooms

Onion

Scallions

Rhubarb

Flowers and herbs

Carnations

Chamomile

Geraniums

Hibiscus

Nasturtium

Pansies

Parsley

Petunias

Roses

Water hyacinth

Vegetables

Beets/beet greens

Bok choy

Broccoli

Dandelion

Mint

Vegetables

Arugula (rocket)

Asparagus

Bell peppers

Cactus pads (nopales)

Carrots

Chicory

Collard greens

Endive

Escarole

Mustard

	Brussels sprouts	greens
	Cabbage	Okra
	Cauliflower	Pea
	Celery	pods/leaves
	Chard	Pumpkin
	Corn	Radicchio
	Cucumber	Squash
	Kale	Sweet
	Lettuces	potatoes
	Peas	Turnip
	Potatoes	greens
	Radishes	Yams
	Spinach	Zucchini

Where to get Vegetation?

Supermarket or grocery store

The most obvious and easiest way for most people to feed a bearded dragon is to simply get extra of the same produce you're cooking for dinner. Organic is the best option if your supermarket offers it. Pesticides and insecticides can be harmful to the long-term health of a lizard, even in small amounts, so if you can't find organic versions be sure to wash the produce thoroughly before use. Don't feed your bearded dragon flowers from the supermarket unless they're specifically sold in the produce department for use as food. The roses in the florist department are often treated with chemicals to make them last longer. The same goes for the blooms from a florist shop.

From your garden

Home-grown food is arguably the safest for your pet, as you can be completely sure any fertilizers or plant food used to grow them don't contain harmful chemicals or compounds. You may find that even if the bulk of your dragon's food comes from the grocery store there are certain things you want to grow yourself. Fresh herbs can be expensive at the store but are easy to grow. Some excellent bearded dragon foods will grow whether you want them to or not. If you live in a temperate region, there are like as not dandelions growing in your front yard. As long as your lawn hasn't been treated, your beardie will be happy to help you take care of that weed problem.

Even if you don't have a yard—or live in a climate where an outdoor garden isn't practical—you can grow some food for your dragon easily within your home. Windowbox herb gardens are available at most home improvement stores. The flowers you feed your beardie can serve double-duty as décor. Geraniums, pansies, and petunias are all known to thrive as houseplants.

Wild collection

Depending on where you live, it may be possible to harvest some of the ingredients you feed your dragon from the surrounding environment. Nopales, for example, grow naturally in parts of the southwestern United States, and those of us in the northeast are likely familiar with dandelion and clover. Make sure you know and trust the area where you're harvesting the plants from. Avoid picking anything growing along the sides of highways. The fuel, oil, and other contaminants in the exhaust of passing vehicles can stick to these plants and make your beardie sick. Whatever berries, herbs, or flowers grow wild in your area, make sure they're correctly identified and thoroughly washed before feeding them to your pet.

Live Food and Protein

Keeping bearded dragons is not a hobby for the squeamish. You will be feeding your dragon live food as a part of his diet. As with the vegetation discussed above, variety is key to your dragon's dietary health, so be prepared to handle and crickets, small worms, and roaches—and, since we're talking about live food, you should be prepared to have habitats of these critters occupying your home.

Live food purchased from a pet store should be "gut loaded" before being fed to your lizard. The food given to feeder insects in most stores is enough to keep them alive but is not nutritionally viable. Gut loading is a process intended to combat this, stuffing the insects full of vitamins and minerals to be passed on to your dragon when he eats them. To make your own gut load at home, use any combination of oatmeal, wheat bran, whole-grain flour, tropical fish food, and rabbit pellets. Throw all the ingredients into the food processor with a pinch each of powdered calcium and vitamin supplement powder and grind into a fine powder. Alternatively, commercial gut loads are available in the reptile section of most pet stores, or can be found online at a very reasonable price. Insects purchased in a pet store should be gut loaded for at least 24 hours before feeding them to your beardie.

None of the insects widely available as food are toxic or harmful to adult bearded dragons. Of more concern are the bugs that may wander into your home and catch your beardie's eye. As a general rule of thumb, don't let your dragon eat anything that's brightly colored, or anything that stings. Especially avoid fireflies, as the compounds that make them glow are highly toxic for a lizard, and eating even one can kill him. Also avoid centipedes, bees and wasps, monarch butterflies, and ladybugs. While bearded dragons eat scorpions and spiders in the wild, it's best to avoid letting him eat spiders he finds in your house. Even arachnids that aren't venomous may be poisonous, and as they're wild animals, you can't be sure what kind of parasites they may be carrying.

The most common live food choices for bearded dragons are crickets, roaches, and worms. Each kind has its own strengths, weaknesses, and unique care requirements. Size is the most important consideration for hatchlings and juveniles. A good rule of thumb is to feed your dragon prey that is no larger in any dimension than the width of your dragon's head. Don't trust the lizard to make this decision on its own. Young dragons, especially, are known for having eyes a bit bigger than their stomachs, and will readily hunt prey far too big to fit in their mouths.

Crickets

By far the most widely-used live food source for lizards, crickets are a good staple protein to serve as the base of your beardie's insect diet. While they're easy to keep alive they're somewhat difficult to raise, so your best bet is to probably buy a few feedings worth at a time from your local pet store, or—for the cheaper option—buying in bulk from an online distributor. They'll usually offer a variety of sizes. Full-grown crickets are no problem for adult beardies, but for hatchlings you'll want to buy the quarter inch size, which might alternatively be labeled as "fly size" or "two weeks old."

Your cricket enclosure can be far more utilitarian in nature than your dragon cage. Some pet stores carry specifically designed cricket cages, typically plastic with tube inserts in the side meant to make it easier to remove the crickets when it's time to feed. These kinds of enclosures are overpriced and ineffective, and a 5.5-gallon aquarium with a screen lid will do just fine. Alternatively, you could use a plastic storage container with a well-fitting lid—provided it's deep enough the crickets won't be able to jump out when you open it. Don't try to store crickets in any kind of cardboard. It will take them a surprisingly short amount of time to chew their way out, and there are few things more frustrating than trying to locate an escaped cricket by the sound of its midnight chirping. The cricket cage shouldn't need daily cleaning, but throw away all the "furnishings" and fully wipe and disinfect it between batches of crickets.

Crickets survive just fine at room temperature, so as long as your home's ambient temperature doesn't drop below 65°F you don't need any heat or light sources. If you're keeping them in a cool space (a basement or a garage in winter) an undertank heater will do fine. To give the crickets somewhere to hide, throw in a couple empty paper towel rolls, egg crates, or pieces of crumpled newspaper. You can put the gut-load in a dish, or just sprinkle it on the bottom of the enclosure. The trickiest part of keeping crickets alive is watering them. They'll have a hard time drinking from a water dish, and will be more likely to drown themselves in the attempt. In the same aisle where you find the commercial gut load you can find artificial cricket drink, taking the form of orange cubes or brightly-colored gel. These products are typically fortified to enhance your gut-loading efforts, but they're also expensive and can have an odd odor, and there's no evidence suggesting their use enhances the nutritional value of feed insects over standard gut loading. The easiest way to water crickets is to cut a slice of juicy fruit or vegetable and place it in the enclosure. Apples, pears, and melons work nicely, as do root vegetables. The moisture in this fruit will be enough to sustain the crickets, and they'll absorb some of the nutrients of the food. Change this fruit slice daily, as part of your salad-making routine.

Roaches

Perhaps the food source people get the oogliest about, roaches are actually the most nutritious widely-available insect option for your dragon. They have a low chitlin content, meaning there's a very low risk of impaction, and they're part of the natural diet of most reptiles. Roaches may be harder to find in some multi-species pet stores but can certainly be purchased from reptile expos or online dealers. The three species most appropriate for bearded dragons are the discoid, the giant lobster, and the orange-spotted, or speckled, roach. None of these can fly (though the giant lobster roach can climb fairly well) and provided you keep them in a well-sealed container, there's significantly less risk of one escaping into your home than there is with crickets.

Roaches can be kept in any solid-sided glass or acrylic aquarium. Fill the bottom with about two inches of potting soil wood mulch as substrate, with paper towel rolls and egg crates for hiding places. Roaches thrive in a warm, wet environment with an ambient temperature of 80-90°F, but they don't need to bask, so an undertank heater will do fine in lieu of an extra heat lamp. Attach the heater to the side of the tank, not the bottom, as the roaches will likely burrow under the substrate and could roast themselves by getting too close to the heat source. Maintain humidity in the enclosure by misting the roaches every day. You can feed them the scraps from your beardie's salads, or with dry dog kibble, tortoise chow, or fish food flakes.

Unlike crickets, it is relatively easy to establish a self-sustaining roach colony, as they will breed if left to their own devices in a suitable environment. This won't happen quickly, though; you may have to wait several months until the colony is large enough for you to begin harvesting.

Mealworms

Mealworms are not the best animal protein source but function well enough as part of a diet balanced by other insect species. Mealworms have a high chitlin content and should not be fed to hatchlings—they've been known to cause paralysis and even death in young beardies. There are a few varieties of mealworms on the market. It's best to go with king mealworms, also called "superworms" or "giant mealworms." These bigger versions are easier to digest than their common cousins (but still should never be given to hatchlings).

Mealworms are hard to raise from eggs, but once you have the larva, it's relatively easy to create a self-sustaining colony. Keep the worms in a container that's at least six inches deep, filled halfway with a gut-loading mixture of oatmeal, whole-grain flour, or wheat bran. Put a few slices of apple or potato in for moisture, replacing every day. Mealworms are the larval stage of the mealworm beetle, and left to their own devices at room temperature, the worms will eventually pupate into adults. These beetles can be fed to your beardie or kept to lay eggs and continue the mealworm colony. Once established, the mealworm enclosure needs little maintenance. Replace the substrate every few months, sifting the beetles and worms out and putting them in a fresh batch. Theoretically you could keep mealworms indefinitely, making them one of the most cost-effective protein food options. Mealworms won't pupate at lower temperatures, so if you'd rather not deal with beetles, simply keep the container in the fridge.

Other Food Options

A quick internet search will reveal that there're a plethora of options for live insect food on the market. You'll rarely find most of these insects at your local pet store and the shipping costs may be prohibitive, but if you're already buying crickets from the site (or you're just curious to try other options) there are several species that work nicely into a beardie's balanced diet.

Most worm and larva species available as feed animals are significantly more nutritious than mealworms. Silkworms are one of the most nutritious feeder insects available. They're expensive and can be difficult to handle but they're chock full of calcium and could be a nice treat for your pregnant females. Silkworms require a very specialized diet of white mulberry leaves; typically, if you order them online, they'll come with a supply of food. Phoenix worms (larval form of black soldier flies) are also high in calcium, and beardies can eat both the larval and adult forms of the animal. If you have hatchlings, flightless fruit flies and flour beetles are nice tiny treats that won't overwhelm their little mouths. Wax worms aren't harmful to bearded dragons, but they are high in fat content, and should be used sparingly if they're fed at all. Also be wary of tomato hornworms, which are the large green caterpillars you can find at some reptile expos. They're large, meaty, and nutritious, but you should only feed them to your dragon if you're sure they were captive bred. Wild tomato hornworms feed on the toxic leaves of the tomato, potato, and tobacco plants, and could pass those toxins on to your beardie.

On the non-worm side, locusts make a wonderful food source for adult bearded dragons. They've got even better nutritional content than crickets and are larger, meaning you won't have to feed so many of them. Since they are larger, however, they take longer to gut load and can be trickier to keep contained, as their powerful legs will allow them to leap out of most enclosures.

Bearded dragons can also be fed mice, though very sparingly (once or twice a month). You should only feed a bearded dragon frozen mice, never live mice, as the teeth and claws of a cornered mouse are plenty to injure a beardie in the tight confines of his enclosure. When you're preparing to offer a mouse to your beardie, make sure it is thoroughly thawed through and at room temperature or warmer. The easiest way to do this is to set it in a warm spot for a couple of hours. The top of the fridge works nicely (just don't forget you put it up there, or you'll have a smelly surprise in a couple days). Mice are high in protein but also high in fat, especially pinkies, the hairless baby mice sold in most pet stores. For this reason, they should be given to healthy dragons only as special treats, though they can be a great help in restoring the health of an underweight dragon.

As mentioned a few times before, your local pet store is the most convenient source of live food. A store that specializes in reptiles or exotic pets, if available, is probably the best in terms of variety and health of the feed animals. Avoid buying worms or other insects at bait shops, even if they have a wider variety of species. These worms are not kept for the purpose of being fed to pets, and you can't be sure what they've been eating or whether they contain any parasites.

Starter colonies of a variety of exotic or hard to find feeder insects can be found either at reptile expos or online. If you're breeding dragons and have hatchlings to feed, you can't beat the price of bulk crickets available on the internet. As technology progresses, this is fast becoming the most effective means of getting live insect food, and these insects are often in better health than the ones you buy at the pet store (some even come already gut loaded). The only issue may be getting crickets in cold weather—most insect providers only guarantee live delivery down to a certain temperature, so if you live in a colder climate, you may need to switch to pet store insects in the winter.

Wild Collection

You can successfully harvest vegetation for your beardie from the surrounding environment, but when it comes to live food, you need to use more caution. There are several reasons for this. First of all, when you bring vegetables home from wherever you've picked them, you invariably wash them. You're not going to be washing the spider or grasshopper you just brought home from the meadow. Plants are stationary, and if you know the area in which they're growing, you can be fairly certain whether they've come into contact with harmful chemicals. Insects are mobile, and even if they're hopping in a clean field, there's no guarantee of what they've brought with them from their last stop. Many insects safely feed on plants that could be toxic to your lizard, absorbing those toxins into their bodies, and you wouldn't know there was a problem until it was too late. Even if they're not directly toxic, wild animals often carry parasites, and these could easily be transferred to your pet. If you're looking to save money on your live food, it's far safer—and ultimately easier—to raise a colony of mealworms or roaches. That being said, you don't have to panic if your beardie snatches a spider while it's out of its cage. Check his droppings over the next few days for irregularities to make sure he hasn't picked up any stomach bugs, and if he comes away clear he should be fine. It's the build-up of toxins over an extended span of eating contaminated insects that poses the biggest threat to a lizard's health.

Bearded dragons need the most protein when they're young and developing, and their insect needs will change drastically as they age. Up to the age of six months, they should be offered insects once or twice a day. Give them about ten small insects in each feeding. Between the ages of six months to a year you can still give your dragon a serving of insects every day, increasing the size of the offerings accordingly. This is the age at which you can introduce pinkie mice or mealworms into the beardie's diet, if you choose to. Once they're fully grown, most of a dragon's nutritional needs are met by vegetables and you can reduce insect feedings to 2-4 times a week.

Monitor your dragon any time you're feeding it live food, keeping track of the prey as much as you're able to. This is a much easier task with mealworms than crickets, though ironically, it's the crickets you really have to worry about. Crickets love to hide under the substrate or in your lizard's hide boxes. If they're left in the cage, they could attack your beardie later on in the day. Even if they don't, they're likely to drown or defecate in your lizard's water dish, creating very unsanitary conditions.

Worms and roaches can be mixed in with your beardie's salad or served in their own designated dish. A cricket's jumping power makes a dish superfluous, so those can simply be tossed into the tank. Only give your beardie as many insects as it can eat in a ten-minute timespan then remove whatever's left over. It's fine if he doesn't eat all of them—he can fill up on his veggies, and due to his desert habitat in the wild, he's well-adapted to skipping a meal or two. The ideal time to give insects to your dragon is about thirty minutes into his "day" (after turning on his heatlamp), but the important thing is consistency. If you have to offer insects to your dragon later in the day, make sure it's at least two hours before turning off the basking lamp for the evening.

Nutritional Supplements

While the most important part of a bearded dragon's nutrition is a well-balanced diet, you can enhance the nutritional value of these foods by adding certain dietary supplements. The best way to give these supplements to your lizard is by dusting them onto the live food you offer. Put half a teaspoon of supplement powder in a jar, sandwich bag, or other sealable container. Drop the insects in, then either shake or roll them around until they've been coated in the powder. Do this immediately before feeding the insects to your dragon so the powder doesn't have a chance to come off.

Dusting the insect food for your beardie is the most effective way to get them extra vitamins, primarily because you can be relatively sure a lizard will eat all of its insects (the same might not be true of its vegetables). Powders put on the vegetable serving also have a tendency to clump up and become too concentrated, which can make them bitter on your dragon's palate and prevent them from eating as many vegetables as they should. You should also avoid putting the powdered supplements in the dragon's water. Being desert animals, bearded dragons drink very little water, and will likely not get a significant amount of nutrition from supplements given this way. Vitamins also have a tendency to decompose or degrade in water, and may promote bacteria growth.

There are two main types of supplements given to bearded dragons: calcium supplements and multivitamins. The details and necessity of each kind of supplement are discussed below.

Calcium Supplements

Especially important for young beardies, you should continue to give calcium supplements even to adult dragons, as it's an important nutrient that's difficult to get through other means. You can find calcium supplements specially formulated for lizards at most pet shops. Be sure to check the label and avoid calcium supplements that also contain phosphorus. Some calcium supplements are fortified with vitamin D3, as well, which is not a necessary part of a calcium supplement but won't hurt.

If you're looking for straight calcium you can also use cuttlebone. Cuttlebone is the internal shell of a cuttlefish and can be found in the bird supply section of most pet stores. Simply break it into small chunks and pulverize it into a powder using a coffee or spice grinder. You can also scrape powder off of the cuttlebone using a knife or file.

Antacid tablets for humans are often made of calcium carbonate and can be used for bearded dragons. Read the ingredients of the tablets before buying them and make sure they don't contain any other medicines. Natural flavoring is fine; your beardie might even enjoy the fruity taste. If you go the antacid route, grind the tablets into a powder the same as you would do with cuttlebone, then dust your insects like you would with other powders. Don't give the whole tablet to a lizard, as this could be an impaction or choking risk.

Hatchlings under six months of age should be given calcium supplements once per day. Juveniles (under a year) should be given four to five calcium supplements a week. Adult bearded dragons should be fine with calcium supplements three times a week, though breeding females should get extra calcium, up to five times per week.

Multi-Vitamin Supplements

Hatchlings and juveniles should be given multi-vitamin supplements once or twice per week. Adults may not need supplements; if you use one, only give it once or twice a month. Multi-vitamins are often high in vitamin A, which can cause toxicity in excessive amounts in an adult dragon, so don't assume more vitamins are always better—you could be doing more harm than good.

Use a multi-vitamin supplement specially formulated for reptiles and amphibians. Lizards require different ratios of vitamins and minerals than humans, and unless you're well-studied in lizard nutrition, it's best to let the experts formulate your supplements. Check the expiration date on any bottle of supplements you buy. Vitamins tend to degrade with time and the pet store may not sell enough reptile supplements to keep a consistently fresh stock. Check the nutritional information and find a supplement with a wide variety of vitamins and minerals, preferably something that includes amino acids. If the supplement contains calcium and phosphorus, make sure they're in a 2:1 ratio. Also look for a supplement that contains little to no vitamin A because of the aforementioned risk of toxicity. If you're not sure what kind of supplement to get, your reptile veterinarian should be able to point you in the right direction.

Watering Your Dragon

Adult bearded dragons are easy to water. Simply provide them with a dish of clean water every day and they'll drink as they get thirsty. When you remove a water dish from the enclosure, dump any remaining water in it down an outside drain or in the toilet, not down the drain in your kitchen sink, to avoid cross-contamination.

It is likely that your bearded dragon will tip over his water dish from time to time. If you're using a sand or recycled paper substrate, you can attempt to combat this by putting the water dish on the bottom of the aquarium and then surrounding it with the substrate (kind of the lizard equivalent of an in-ground pool). If the water bowl is toppled, you want to clean it up as soon as you notice it. Remove, clean, and refill the dish, then remove any moistened substrate from the cage. Spilled water can very quickly turn to humidity, especially in a glass enclosure, and elevated humidity for a long period of time can lead to respiratory infections in bearded dragons.

Hatchlings can be more difficult to water than their adult counterparts, as they are prone to both dehydration and drowning. The best way to keep them hydrated is to provide only a very shallow water container (large jar lids work wonderfully for this, filled to a depth of less than one inch) and then mist the hatchling dragons once or twice a day using clean water in a spray bottle. This will also help the hatchlings shed, which they'll be doing a lot as their young bodies grow.

Chapter 5: Health and Breeding

As mentioned before, bearded dragons are hardy lizards that aren't prone to many ailments or illnesses. Most of the ailments that do affect them can be avoided with proper care and nutrition. A healthy dragon is active and curious, with a body weight between 300 and 500 grams. Unless pregnant, the dragon's stomach should not drag on the ground; this is a sign of obesity, and should be corrected by limiting the dragon's food intake and at least temporarily eliminating mice and sugary fruits. A healthy dragon has few recurring health needs, though you might need to occasionally trim his nails, and should be aware of his shedding and brumation cycles. Remember that regular veterinary check-ups are an important part of a bearded dragon's health. Check the listings on the Association of Reptile and Amphibian Veterinarians (www.arav.org) if you're not sure where to find a reptile vet in your area.

Nail Trimming

Most of the time, a bearded dragon's claws are sufficiently worn down by walking over cage furnishings. You don't need to trim the nails unless you notice them curling back toward the body along the underside of the toe. Your vet can trim your dragon's claws if you don't feel comfortable. If you're trimming your dragon's nails yourself, you can use either bird or cat claw trimmers. Trim a very small amount at a time and use a nail file to smooth out cracked or rough edges. There's a fleshy part inside most animal nails, known as the quick, and you want to avoid trimming so much of the claw that you hit this—trimming the hard parts of the nails won't hurt your dragon, but nicking the quick will. Keep something nearby to staunch the bloodflow in case you do accidentally trim too deep. A wet teabag works well for this, or an absorbent powder like flour or cornstarch. Dab some antibiotic ointment on the nail once it stops bleeding and keep an eye on it to make sure it doesn't get infected.

Shedding

Your dragon will shed periodically. Unlike snakes, which shed in one large piece of skin, bearded dragons shed in bits and pieces. Young, quickly-growing beardies will shed more often than adults. While he's shedding, your dragon may eat less or be more irritable, so it's best not to handle him much. If you want to help the shedding along you can mist the cage a few times or give your lizard a bath in one or two inches of warm water. Moisture softens the skin and helps it fall off more easily. Don't pull off any skin. It'll fall of when it's ready, and pulling it off before that could cause abrasions. If there are stray scraps of dry skin left on the dragon's toes or the tip of his tail once he's finished you can soak your dragon and gently rub the skin off with your fingers.

Brumation

Similar to hibernation, brumation is a process bearded dragons in the wild use to survive the winter. During brumation, a dragon digs a deep burrow and enters a state of torpor to conserve energy until the spring. You can tell brumation is about to happen because your dragon will get very sluggish and eat less (or even stop eating entirely). He'll also spend less time basking, preferring the cooler end of his cage; he may hang out in his hide box all day or burrow down into the substrate. This is the main way you'll know if he's sick or entering brumation, because a sick beardie will spend more time basking than usual.

In captivity, bearded dragons may or may not enter brumation. Some enter the state in some years and not others. If it does happen, you shouldn't be alarmed—which is good, because there's nothing you can do to stop it. Once brumation starts, the best thing you can do for your dragon is set him up a vet appointment. If there are any parasites or latent illnesses in his system they may proliferate and attack while his body's defenses are shut down. You can also help him along by simulating winter, reducing daylight hours to as little as 8-10 per day (you can raise it back to normal levels when he's finished). It's hard to tell how long the brumation period will last. It could mean you can't wake your dragon up for 2-3 months; it could mean he spends a few weeks taking long naps and being especially sluggish when he's awake. However long the brumation lasts, check on him periodically. If you're concerned that the dragon is dehydrated (loose and wrinkled skin is a sign of this) you can put him in a container with about an inch of warm water on the bottom for about fifteen minutes. He may or may not drink, but the moisture will help either way.

If you want to breed your dragons, you might want to induce brumation. Breeding is triggered in dragons by the coming of spring (warmth and heat) after a long span of cold and dark. To trigger brumation, you can adjust the photoperiod for your lizards down to 8-10 hours a day, like it would be in winter back home. Even if no brumation cycle is triggered, this simulated winter should trigger mating behaviors once it's over.

Common Health Ailments

Diagnosing health problems with a lizard—or even figuring out that something is wrong—can sometimes be difficult. Look for aberrations in his behavioral patterns. As mentioned above, sick bearded dragons will often give themselves a "fever," raising their core body temperature by basking longer than usual to kill off the invading micro-organisms. If you notice him doing this, you can help the process by increasing the temperature of your light by up to ten degrees, though you should still set up a vet appointment as soon as possible to discover the root of the issue.

Changes to the lizard's stool are often a good indicator of internal parasites. If your dragon's waste is noticeably runny, oddly colored, or smells worse than usual—and there have been no major changes to his diet—you should consult your veterinarian. Other signs of a problem are the same ones you'd look for when shopping for your lizard—swellings and discolorations on the body, discharge from the nose or eyes, and an unnatural gait, especially dragging either hindlimb. Read on for a more in-depth look at some of the most common ailments affecting bearded dragons.

Parasites

Occasionally, your bearded dragon may pick up either internal or external parasites. External parasites are easier to diagnose and treat. The most common ones are mites and ticks. Ticks are blood-sucking insects that feed on a variety of animals. If you see one on your dragon, don't just pull it off. Often the mouth parts will get stuck under the skin and lead to infection. You can coat the tick with petroleum jelly or dust it with an insecticide powder (like Sevin) then pluck it off with tweezers when the tick has died.

Mites look like tiny black or brown dots and are often found around a lizard's eyes. You'll often learn your lizard has mites because you'll see them drowned in his water dish (they'll look like dirt at the bottom). The mites that infest bearded dragons will only feed on lizards, so don't worry about contracting them from your pet. While it's best to make an appointment with your vet if you notice mites, it may be possible to take care of mites at home. You can find mite sprays designed for reptiles with Ivermectin as a base at most pet supply stores. Read and carefully follow all instructions on the bottle exactly, and remove the permanent water dish while you're treating your lizard with insecticide to avoid contaminating his water source. Most reptile experts suggest spraying the reptile and his environment every 3-5 days, for a period of up to eight weeks. Your vet might give you different care instructions. It's important to complete the entire recommended treatment cycle, even if there are no more visible traces of the mites, to make sure all traces of the infestation are gone. Avoid "no-pest strips" with an active ingredient of Vapona or dichlorvos. While some breeders recommend and use these products, they have also been indicated in the deaths of a variety of species.

Internal parasites can be harder to diagnose. If your beardie has worms, you'll often see them moving in his stool. Changes to a lizard's stool are the best indication of a parasite infestation. Other signs include bloating, vomiting, constipation, weight loss, and sluggishness. A reptile vet will be able to identify and suggest treatment for internal parasites. While your lizard is under treatment, it's best to change his substrate to newspaper or paper towels and remove any wooden cage furnishings (or those made of other porous materials) to prevent the parasites from hiding out and re-occurring.

There are a couple species of internal parasite worthy of a special notice. Coccidia is a digestive parasite so common in beardies it's actually considered normal for them to have it. In reasonable amounts, it's not harmful to a dragon and may aid in his digestion. It becomes a problem only if the organisms proliferate. This is often caused by long-term environmental stress or another illness (coccidia proliferation can also be an issue following brumation, another reason it's a good idea to take your beardie for a check-up before and after his brumation cycle). Diarrhea, weight loss, and dehydration are signs that your dragon's suffering from an excess of coccidia, though it will most often be diagnosed in conjunction with another problem. Coccidia is resistant to bleach, so if your lizard undergoes treatment you should disinfect his cage furnishings with a 10% ammonia solution, using the same process outlined for bleach disinfecting in chapter 2.

On the other end of the spectrum is cryptosporidiosis (or "crypto"), a very dangerous internal parasite known to affect several reptile species. Cypto can be transmitted from lizards to humans and vice versa. In humans, it will usually appear two to ten days after infection and can last from two weeks to a month. Diarrhea is the most common and consistent symptom, though patients frequently also experience nausea, vomiting, fever symptoms consistent with a severe stomach flu. Crypto is rarely fatal in human beings with a healthy immune system but can be especially dangerous for AIDS patients, cancer patients undergoing chemotherapy, infants, and the elderly.

The effects of crypto on a reptile can be devastating. Crypto has what's known as a direct life cycle, meaning the eggs of the next round of organisms are contained in the animal's stool and can easily re-transmit into the body. A reptile suffering from crypto should be kept in a bare-bones enclosure with no permanent water source. Change the entire substrate any time you notice waste. Wear disposable gloves while caring for a lizard with crypto, and wash your hands well after every encounter.

Cryptosporidiosis has similar warning signs to other lizard ailments—swelling of the abdomen, sluggishness, and vomiting or diarrhea. Left untreated it can lead to dehydration, seizures, paralysis, and eventually death. Treatment is possible if it's caught early, but there's no cure for the disease caused by prolonged crypto exposure and humane euthanization may be the best remaining option if left for too long.

Impaction

Caused by foreign matter lodged in the intestinal tract, impaction can be life-threatening but is also easily treated and entirely preventable. Most instances of impaction are caused by eating unsuitable substrates or inedible objects, like fruit seeds or plastic from shoddy cage furnishings. It could also be caused by a build-up of insect shells, or by eating bugs that are too big, and is the main reason mealworms should be avoided as food for hatchling dragons. A low basking site temperature reduces a dragon's digestive functions, and can also contribute to impaction.

Constipation is the first sign of impaction. If your dragon has been eating but hasn't produced waste in 2-3 days, feel his abdomen for any unusual lumps or hard deposits. A vet can usually solve an impaction problem by administering an enema; in severe cases, surgery may be required. After setting up your vet appointment, you may be able to relieve impaction by giving your beardie a few drops of vegetable oil then bathing him in 1-2 inches of warm water while you gently massage his abdomen. Keep the vet appointment even if he passes the blockage to make sure there're no traces of the impacting material remaining.

Metabolic Bone Disorder

Metabolic Bone Disorder (MBD) is a weakening of the skeletal structure caused by calcium deficiency. MBD can be prevented with a proper diet (high in calcium and vitamin D3, low in phosphorus) and adequate exposure to UVB light. Unusual bends or curves in a dragon's limbs or spine are the first sign of MBD. As the disease progresses, it will begin to affect the bones of the face and jaw, causing swelling at the jawline and spontaneous bone fractures. Luckily, the effects of MBD can be reversed if caught in an early enough stage of the disease. Work with your veterinarian to develop a more effective care plan. This will likely involve altering your dragon's diet and lighting.

Respiratory infections

Respiratory infections develop in bearded dragons when they're kept in enclosures that are too humid or too cool. Symptoms are similar to those of a human cold, and include discharge from the nostrils, sneezing, wheezing, and a general lack of energy. Increase the temperature at the basking site by up to ten degrees to help your beardie fight the infection, and consider altering your cage to prevent future infections. This may mean reducing the size of the water dish, relocating the water dish into a cooler area of the cage, improving the cage's ventilation, or decreasing the distance between the heat source and the basking site.

Egg Binding

Only affecting female dragons, egg binding results when a gravid dragon is unable to lay her eggs and retains them in her body. Your female may produce eggs even if no male is present. They'll be infertile and won't hatch, but she'll still need to lay them. Be especially mindful of this after your female dragon comes out of brumation as this typically triggers mating behaviors in both genders. When eggs are bound, they can rupture and cause an infection, or calcify, causing injury to the reproductive system. You can help prevent this by providing your female a suitable egg laying location (see more about this in the breeding section) but if she still won't or can't lay her eggs, surgery may be required. If you do not plan on breeding your female dragon and want to prevent this from happening, she can be spayed by a reptile vet.

Mouth Rot

Officially known as stomatitis, mouth rot is a gum infection that can result in tooth loss or the death of bone tissue when left untreated. Mouth rot is found most frequently in dragons kept in dirty enclosures with insufficient heat. Poor diet is often also a contributing factor. Signs of mouth rot include redness or swelling of the mouth lining and gums, a distorted jaw, or a lack of interest in food. You may also see cheesy deposits around the dragon's teeth. While it can be treated with an antibiotic, your vet will likely also ask you to make some changes to your beardie's living conditions.

Other issues

Bearded dragons occasionally suffer from vitamin A toxicity, generally caused by overuse of vitamin supplements. Signs of vitamin A overdose include a swelling throat, bloating, and sluggishness. Vitamin A toxicity can be treated with medical care and adjustments to the diet.

If your dragon falls from a substantial height, monitor him closely after for any changes to his gait or activity level, and contact your vet immediately if anything seems off.

Burns can also be a serious problem if left untreated. These can be caused by an undertank heater that's too hot or a basking lamp that's too close. If you use a light fixture set atop a wire mesh screen, remember that the wire mesh under the heater is going to get nearly as hot as the bulb itself. Wash all burns and dab with antiseptic ointment, keeping a close watch on them. Call your vet at any sign of infection. You should also locate the source of the burn and adjust the enclosure accordingly.

It's been illegal to export bearded dragons from Australia for the pet trade since the 1960s, so in any other country where you can buy bearded dragons there's a long-established history of successful breeding. This means amateur breeders have a much greater access to information and knowledge than with most lizard species, whose captive breeding programs may have only begun within the past ten or so years. This does not mean breeding is a good idea for every lizard owner, and you should research the topic carefully before deciding to breed your dragon.

Male bearded dragons can begin breeding at 18 months, but it's best with females to wait until they're two years old to make sure the skeleton is fully developed—the egg creation process takes a lot of calcium out of a female dragon's body. The most important thing when you're getting ready to breed any lizard is to make sure both parent animals are in perfect health. You also need to make sure you are capable of taking care of both the parents and the eggs. If you're starting from a single dragon, this means adding a second 55-gallon tank for the partner. Do not plan on cohabitating a mating pair of bearded dragons in the long-term. Even if they're given enough space to avoid territorial squabbles, the male is likely to overbreed the female if kept with her permanently. Egg production takes a lot out of a female's body, and overbreeding can cause permanent and irreversible health problems.

You will also need some kind of external, temperature-controlled container for the egg incubation and a place to put the hatchlings. And there will be a lot of hatchlings—female dragons typically lay 20-30 eggs at a time. Even if you plan on selling the dragons, you won't be able to safely do this until they're about four months of age, so be sure you have both the time and the money to take care of a couple dozen hungry dragon babies for at least that long. Baby bearded dragons can be housed together more effectively than adults, but you should still plan on keeping no more than 5-6 individuals in the same enclosure. Hatchling beardies are also eating machines, capable of putting away as many as 60-70 small crickets every day. Keeping a breeding pair of bearded dragons plus their hatchlings means somewhere in the neighborhood of seven total enclosures to maintain, and a per-week consumption of around 500 crickets per hatchling dragon (that's 10,000 crickets a week if your beardie has twenty babies!) plus all the salad and supplements.

If that thought gives you pause, you may want to reconsider breeding your bearded dragon.

If you've read the above and are confident you have the time, space, and resources, then you're ready to get started.

If you only have one dragon now, you'll need someone for him or her to breed with. Buying a full-grown adult is the best way to make sure the dragon is the correct gender to breed with yours. Dragons breed best with other individuals that are roughly the same size and weight, so keep that in mind when shopping for your dragon's partner. Once you get the new pet home, quarantine it for a period of at least two weeks before introducing it to your established dragon to avoid spreading any parasites that came home with your new beardie.

Introducing the Dragons

As territorial as they are, introducing bearded dragons to each other can be a delicate and lengthy process. Don't just plop them in the cage together and expect them to get along. Once you're sure the new dragon is healthy, you should schedule a supervised meeting. It's probably easiest to introduce the female into the male enclosure. If the dragons start to fight, the male will be the more aggressive and it will be easier to handle and remove the female. Looking out for signs of aggression during this introduction can be tricky. A lot of a male dragon's aggressive behaviors— like head bobbing or enlarging and darkening of the beard—are also mating displays meant to attract female attention. Take note of these displays, but you don't necessarily have to remove the dragon unless the two begin to bite at each other. Even if they're getting along great, limit this first visit to about an hour so you don't cause undue stress to either dragon. Repeat this process every day for a week, gradually

157

lengthening the amount of time the dragons are together. Carefully check your dragons for injuries in case they're nipping each other while you're not looking. Make sure the male is allowing the female to bask and that they're both getting access to food. If you feel any trepidation about leaving them alone together after this first week, go with that instinct. Sometimes beardie couples simply don't get along. Trying to force the matter will only put undue stress on both animals.

Brumation

In the wild, breeding behaviors are triggered by brumation through a cold, dark winter, followed by emerging into a bright, hot spring. You can simulate this cycle in your bearded dragon enclosures by reducing the amount of sunlight to 8-10 hours per day for a span of 2-3 months (more specifics about brumation are discussed earlier in the chapter). You'll know if the male is ready to mate after this process because his beard will darken and he'll be more active, displaying more territorial and mating behaviors.

Mating

Once your dragons have recovered from brumation and are back to being their curious, heat-loving selves, it's time to let the happy couple move in together. Put the female in the male's tank for a full week, then remove her for a full week. Then do it again—a week with the male, a week alone. Return the female to the male's cage for a third week, then remove her permanently to her own enclosure and provide her with an egg box if you've witnessed successful copulations.

To attract the female, the male bearded dragon will puff up his beard and stamp his foot on the ground while bobbing his head. If receptive, the female will lower her body, perhaps bobbing her head back and waving a forelimb in a circle toward the male as a sign of submission. The male dragon will then chase the female around the cage until she fully submits and mount her from behind. He may bite her neck during this process; this is normal and shouldn't be a cause for concern. The entire process, from displaying through copulation, can take place in less than five minutes—an important thing to keep in mind if you want to have your dragons out playing together when you're not trying to mate them.

Laying the Eggs

While she's carrying eggs, the female will be plumper than usual. You may even be able to see the outline of the eggs through her skin—they'll look like round protrusions about the size of marbles. Her behavior will change as she gets closer to laying. She'll eat less, perhaps eating nothing in the day or two before starting to lay. Right before she starts to lay she'll start digging rather aggressively in the corners of her cages, looking for a safe place for her eggs. The female will begin laying her eggs about four to six weeks after mating. You should provide her a with a good nesting site where she can do this, some kind of pan or tub set into her cage floor at an angle to allow easy access. Fill the tub with at least six inches of moist sand or potting soil. Your beardie may not lay her eggs if she doesn't have a suitable site, causing her to become egg bound. It may take her up to a month to lay her full batch of eggs, so don't panic if she doesn't seem to be laying them all unless she starts to act lethargic or depressed. Remove the eggs to an incubator as she lays them, and give your female extra calcium and insects during and immediately after the egg laying process. Even when provided with a perfect lay box she may lay a few of her eggs elsewhere in the enclosure, so pay extra close attention to cage corners especially when you're cleaning her cage during this process. If left in the cage, these eggs will likely rot, causing potential bacteria build-up.

In rare cases, female beardies lay multiple clutches in one breeding season. If this happens, the second clutch will come around 4-6 weeks after the first. If you notice your beardie looking gravid again (swollen abdomen, eggs visible under the skin) dramatically increase how much food you offer her, focusing on increasing her calcium. Pinkie mice might be great for her at this point, or wax worms and other foods you'd typically avoid because they're too high in fat.

Incubation and Hatching

Set up your incubator before your dragon starts laying so that the eggs can be removed immediately. You can use an avian incubator (or hovbator) as long as it's got precise temperature controls. You could also make your own incubator in a spare terrarium. Dragon eggs require a lower temperature than the dragons themselves, ideally about 84°F, plus or minus three degrees. If the temperature gets above 90°F it's likely to kill the developing embryos. The relative humidity should also be higher than with a bearded dragon, around 75-80%.

Vermiculite is far and away the most recommended substrate for incubating dragon eggs. It looks a bit like mulch, or pale dirt, but it's actually made from the mineral mica, and is fantastic for incubating eggs because of how much moisture it can hold. You can find vermiculite at most home and garden stores. If you're using a commercial incubator, either give each egg its own deli cup (with holes poked in the lid for ventilation) or put a few side by side in a Tupperware container. Fill the container about halfway with vermiculite that's been mixed with water until it clumps (but doesn't drip) when squeezed. If you're using a converted terrarium, an undertank heater is the best way to maintain temperature without producing any hot spots. Fill the terrarium with a few inches of vermiculite. In either case, eggs should be about half-buried when they start—you can make depressions for them in the vermiculite with your thumb. Healthy eggs will grow as they develop, sometimes even doubling in size, so don't overcrowd them.

Fresh dragon eggs are relatively firm, but you should still use care when extracting them from the cage. Gently dig them up with your fingers or a plastic spoon. Don't feel bad removing the eggs or think your female beardie will be sad to be separated from her children. The truth is, bearded dragons lack any kind of maternal instinct, and the adult is more likely to eat the eggs than to care for them. In either case, a dragon terrarium is not the best place to incubate eggs, and you're unlikely to get many (if any) hatchlings from the batch if they're left with mom.

When you remove the eggs, try to keep them oriented the same way they were when you found them. This doesn't become especially important until the embryos inside the egg have started to develop (turning the eggs at this point can kill the baby inside) but even so it's best to keep them right-side up. Some breeders mark the top of the egg with a pencil to prevent them from being turned during transfer.

Healthy, fertilized eggs will be a matte white color as they develop. At the late stages, you may even be able to see the baby dragons moving around inside. Eggs that are other colors may be infertile but it's best to leave them in the incubator until you're sure. The eggs may begin to mold as they're incubating. Advice on dealing with this varies from expert to expert. If the molding egg is obviously not developing (eg it's a strange color, it's not growing, etc) you might as well remove and discard it; if the egg is otherwise healthy you should be fine leaving it in, as there's no proof mold affects hatchability.

Eggs can take anywhere from 5-12 weeks to hatch. You'll know hatching is imminent because the eggs will begin to deflate and may "sweat" small drops of moisture. Once the baby beardie slices the shell open with his egg tooth, he'll pop his head out and then often stop to rest. It can take a healthy beardie up to 36 hours to fully emerge from his egg. Don't try to help him. Hatchlings are very delicate, and you'll likely end up hurting him. Leave the baby beardie in the incubator for about a day after he's fully emerged to give him time to get used to life. The presence of a baby may also stimulate the other eggs to hatch. Most of the babies will emerge within a day or two of each other, but it can take up to a week from the first hatching to the last, so don't assume the remaining eggs are dead until a bit of time has passed.

Care of the Hatchlings

Baby beardie habitats are essentially tweaked versions of their parents'. Babies need the same heat but a higher humidity. Favor flat substrates, like newspaper or paper towels, and mist the dragons once or twice a day instead of giving them a permanent water dish—baby beardies may drown, even in very shallow water. The yolk of the baby's egg will sustain it for a little while after hatching, so you shouldn't start to offer food until they're 3-4 days old. Remember that these little guys are about three inches from snout to tail and adjust their food accordingly. They'll eat a lot but it has to be small. Cut up all vegetables into very fine pieces (a few "whirs" of the food processor can't hurt) and remember the rule of thumb from the feeding chapter: No live food bigger in any dimension than the width of the dragon's head. Make greens constantly available and give them crickets or other small insects 2-3 times a day. You can house the hatchlings communally at first, but they should be separated out into smaller and smaller groups as they grow. Sort the dragons by size, keeping the bigger ones together, so the runts don't miss out on the nutrients they need. By the time they're four months old you should have no more than 5-6 individuals in the same enclosure.

This is just a basic overview of the breeding practices used to best effect by professional bearded dragon keepers. If you're serious about breeding your dragons, you should expand upon this knowledge by doing your own research. Books and internet forums are a good place to start, but you can't beat the real-world advice you could get from a professional breeder. A trip to the next reptile expo in your area will be the best place to find a concentrated wealth of knowledge on best breeding practices.

Additional Resources

For additional reading, I recommend these two internet forums:

https://www.beardeddragon.org/forums/

http://www.beardeddragonforum.com/